The Way We Drove

The Way We Drove

Toronto's love affair

with the automobile

in stories

and photographs

Bill Sherk

Stoddart   A Boston Mills Press Book

Canadian Cataloguing in Publication Data

Sherk, Bill, 1942–
The way we drove: Toronto's love affair with the automobile in stories and photographs

Includes bibliographic references.
ISBN 1-55046-065-x

1. Automobiles – Ontario – Toronto – History.
I. Title.

TL27.T67S54   1993   388.3'42'09713541   C93-093682-5

First published in 1993 by
Stoddart Publishing Co. Limited
34 Lesmill Road
Toronto, Canada
M3B 2T6
(416) 445-3333

A BOSTON MILLS PRESS BOOK
The Boston Mills Press
132 Main Street
Erin, Ontario
N0B 1T0

Book design by Counterpunch/Linda Gustafson
Set in Monotype Walbaum (revived in 1933) and Koloss (first
released in 1930)
Printed in Canada

The publisher gratefully acknowledges the support of the
Canada Council,
Ontario Ministry of Culture and Communications, Ontario Arts
Council and
Ontario Publishing Centre in the development of writing and
publishing in Canada.

Dedication

To my wife, Brenda, whose love and encouragement made this book possible.

Table of Contents

Part Two:

Between the Wars, 1918–1939

25

Part Three:

From Rumble Seats to Fuel Injection, 1939–1957

67

Introduction

Imagine sitting in a traffic jam in downtown Toronto sixty years ago, surrounded by Studebakers, LaSalles, Packards, DeSotos, Durants, Hudsons, Gray-Dorts, Hupmobiles, Overlands, McLaughlin-Buicks, Model A Fords, and a horse-drawn milk wagon. Your passengers in the rumble seat tell you to get moving or they'll be late for work. You blow the OOGAH horn on your Whippet roadster, but the cars ahead refuse to budge. Your rad starts boiling over. Then a loud BANG from behind tells you that patched-up used tire you put on the left rear has just blown its inner tube. Cursing, you open the door and step off the running board into a warm, fresh pile of "road apples." Yes, it's going to be another great day on the streets of Hogtown!

PART ONE

The First Twenty-Five Years, 1893–1918

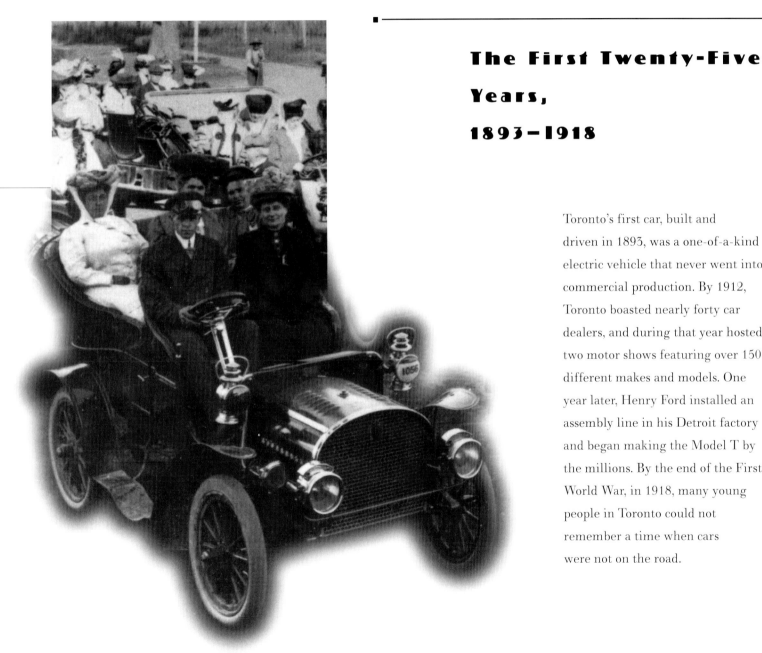

Toronto's first car, built and driven in 1893, was a one-of-a-kind electric vehicle that never went into commercial production. By 1912, Toronto boasted nearly forty car dealers, and during that year hosted two motor shows featuring over 150 different makes and models. One year later, Henry Ford installed an assembly line in his Detroit factory and began making the Model T by the millions. By the end of the First World War, in 1918, many young people in Toronto could not remember a time when cars were not on the road.

Where It All Began

Toronto's love affair with the automobile began on the
northeast corner of Bay and Temperance in 1893, when John
Dixon's Carriage Works (seen here on November 5, 1900)
constructed an electric-powered vehicle for Toronto patent
attorney Frederick Barnard Fetherstonhaugh. The car's batteries and motor were designed by a British-born Toronto
electrician named William Still, who had been working on
the development of self-propelled electric vehicles for some

time. When he finally came up with the lightweight,
energy-efficient battery he had been searching for, he
approached Fetherstonhaugh to secure a patent.

Fetherstonhaugh was impressed. He took a keen interest
in all the latest inventions of the day and was particularly
intrigued with the future possibilities of electricity. His
mansion at Mimico Point, just west of Toronto, was one of
the first homes in Canada to get electric lights, and he had
plenty of money to pour into an electric car. He and Still
quickly came to an understanding: Still's batteries and motor

would be used in the construction of a smooth, silent, high-quality horseless carriage that would be put together for Fetherstonhaugh by the J. Dixon Carriage Works.

Fetherstonhaugh was delighted with the finished product, which had many features years ahead of their time, including electric lights, pneumatic tires, and a folding top. He demonstrated his unique vehicle in 1893 at the CNE (then called the Toronto Industrial Exhibition), where he took nervous dignitaries for a ride around a circular track in front of the old grandstand.

For the next fifteen years or so, Fetherstonhaugh drove his pride and joy around the city. The 700-pound vehicle could travel at 15 miles per hour for up to an hour. The resourceful owner obtained permission from the Toronto & York Radial Railway Company to recharge his batteries by hooking onto the trolley wires running past his home at Lakeshore Boulevard and Church Street (now Royal York Road), then later bought his own stationary gasoline engine and generator. The car was featured at the first Toronto Motor Show in 1906, and the accompanying photograph was taken at a motor show at the Toronto Armouries on University Avenue around 1912. Fetherstonhaugh apparently sold the car sometime after that, and what became of it is not known. Perhaps a lucky treasure hunter will some day find it stashed away in an old garage.

And what became of the Dixon Carriage Works, which built the car in 1893? It continued to manufacture horse-drawn carriages and survived well into the twentieth century, then re-established its connection with cars when it became a Nash showroom in 1920. It was demolished the following year to make room for the General Assurance Building, which still occupies the site at 357 Bay Street.

THE FIRST MOTOR VEHICLE MADE AND OPERATED IN CANADA BUILT IN 1893

5

"This carriage was built for F.B. Fetherstonhaugh in 1893 by John Dixon and equipped by the Still Motor Co., afterwards the Canadian Motor Co. Limited, with Motor and Batteries made by W. W. Still. It was exhibited in the Toronto Exhibition in 1893 and created quite a sensation in front of the Old Grandstand on account of it being the first Horseless Vehicle made or operated in Canada."

When the above sign was displayed on the front of the Fetherstonhaugh car at the Toronto Motor Show around 1912, the car was generally believed to be "the first Horseless Vehicle made or operated in Canada." But nearly fifty years later – in 1960 – the remains of a steam buggy dating from 1867 were discovered in an attic in Stanstead, Quebec. That car has since been restored and now resides at the National Museum of Science and Technology in Ottawa. But the Fetherstonhaugh car still carries the distinction of being the oldest car built and driven in Toronto. It has now been immortalized on the 1993 Canadian $100 gold coin.

More Cars Soon Followed

As the 1890s turned into the 1900s, a variety of horseless carriages began sharing the muddy streets of Hogtown with Fetherstonhaugh's pride and joy.

Henry Pellatt, who was later to build (and ultimately be bankrupted by) Casa Loma, owned one of the first electric vehicles in Toronto – and because the city would not have traffic lights until years later (1925), he was able to drive more or less non-stop down to his favourite hangout, the University Avenue Armouries, to visit his favourite regiment, the Queen's Own Rifles. When he pulled into the parking lot, he continued driving non-stop because he didn't know how to bring his car to a halt. Round and round he went, no doubt bellowing in panic, until some of the soldiers threw a pile of hay in front of his car.

In her fascinating book, *The Toronto Story*, Claire Mackay describes the beginnings of speed regulation: "By 1902, cars were so common Toronto rewrote its traffic laws. The speed limit was 15 miles an hour in the city, unless you were within 100 yards of a horse-drawn vehicle, in which case it was seven miles an hour. If your car scared a horse, you had to pull into a sidestreet, park, and go back and calm it down, or be fined $25."

Some cars of that day were pushed more than driven, and the wise motorist was always prepared for the worst when taking the car out for a spin. One man in Toronto attached an iron ring to the back of his car to lead his horse behind him as a built-in "tow truck" whenever he went out for a drive. As if that were not enough, he was planning to install a whiffletree (the swinging bar to which the traces of a harness are fastened) at the front, but died before he got the chance.

A mechanical breakdown often led to the embarrassment of having to sit in your car as it was towed by a horse to the nearest blacksmith shop, where if you were lucky a replacement part could be forged on the anvil. Many affluent early car owners hired chauffeurs who were also skilled as mechanics.

Fixing a flat on this 1917 McLaughlin-Buick was no easy task. The front seat has been taken out, probably because the tools were stashed under it. Drivers back then were lucky to get a thousand miles from a set of tires, and many cars carried two spares.

The roads in those days were littered with horseshoe nails that chewed your tires to pieces, and you could easily run out of gas miles from the nearest hardware store, where gasoline was dispensed from gallon cans and poured into your tank through a chamois to catch the impurities. Before the arrival of the motor car, gasoline had been a useless and dangerous byproduct of kerosene, and the British-American Oil Company dumped the stuff into the Don River until motorists began paying money for it.

The three sources of power for motor vehicles around the turn of the century were electricity, steam, and gasoline. Electric cars were smooth and quiet, but travelled at only moderate speeds and required frequent recharging. Steam cars (such as the Stanley Steamer) needed time to build up steam pressure, and many people thought the boiler might explode (even though it was wrapped in piano wire). Gasoline cars were noisy and dirty, but they started in a hurry and could easily be modified to go faster. By the time Henry Ford began building the Model T in October 1908, gasoline was emerging as the power source of the future.

You Push and I'll Steer

Traditional turn-of-the-century sex roles are illustrated in this photo taken on the outskirts of Toronto and now preserved in the City of Toronto Archives. The car is a Stephens, built in England between 1898 and 1900 by R. Stephens, a Clevedon, Somerset, cycle engineer who built about a dozen of these 8-horsepower twin-cylinder cars with belt and chain drive and independent suspension. The front of the car clearly shows the influence of bicycle technology. Note the squeeze horn conveniently mounted on the steering tiller. The fate of the car shown here is unknown, but the Stephens prototype has survived.

Speed King of the World

Barney Oldfield became a household name in 1902 when he raced Henry Ford's "999" at the Grosse Pointe Track near Detroit. He won, and the publicity generated by that victory helped to launch the Ford Motor Company the following year. In that same year (1903), Oldfield roared around the dirt oval at Indianapolis in the "999" racer he had bought from Henry Ford, and reportedly became the first man to go a mile a minute.

In 1904, he raced through the United States and Canada in his Peerless Green Dragon, while dressed in a matching all-leather suit, and smashed all records over distances from 1 to 50 miles as the crowds cheered him on. On Saturday, August 6 of that year, a frenzy of excitement swept through the CNE grandstand in Toronto as Barney crouched low over the wheel, stepped on the gas, and slid through the turns. Fergus Kyle covered the event from atop the grandstand for the *Canadian Magazine:* "It was really startling. A man could take a match from his pocket as the auto passed the starting point, strike it and light his pipe, take an extra puff to make sure it was going, and look up to find the machine half-way round the half-mile track; would just have time to shift his position for a good look at the finish, when it would shoot past with a devilish rattle."

After leaving Toronto, Oldfield continued piling up victory

after victory, winning his most cherished title, "Speed King of the World," on March 16, 1910, on the hard sand beaches of Daytona, where his 200-horsepower Blitzen Benz set a world land speed record of 131.7 miles per hour!

Oldfield retired from racing in 1918 and died in 1946. He was elected to the Auto Racing Hall of Fame in 1953. This photo shows Barney Oldfield and his adoring fans in Toronto, in August 1904.

Twenty-Five Cents, Please

These gentlemen, including the police officer, are posing for the camera around 1904 at the east entrance of the Toronto Industrial Exhibition (renamed the Canadian National Exhibition in 1912), in the present-day vicinity of the Prince's Gates, erected in 1927. The man behind the tiller is driving a Northern automobile (see page 12) and will have to pay 25 cents admission to get in – a price that remained unchanged until 1949! Perhaps he was one of the many thrill-seekers who came to watch the death-defying driving skills of "speed king" Barney Oldfield (previous photo).

I Must Get One of Those

An early touring car (number 7623) bumps along an un-paved Yonge Street around 1910. The passengers on the rear platform of streetcar number 1272 appear to be staring at the car with a mixture of envy and curiosity. They might be thinking the car is the "better way" and wondering when they will be able to afford one.

Out for a Drive Around 1905

Toronto motorists with families and friends enjoy an outing in automobiles still too primitive for windshields or tops (except for the canopied vehicle in the background). Hats and caps were de rigueur in Edwardian Toronto, and a couple of drivers can be seen with goggles. Corsets lined with whalebone gave many women a shape that nature did not. (Note the bosomy hourglass figure in left background.)

Until 1905 licence plates were made of leather and hung from the rear, but the number was also painted on one or both of the cowl lights facing the front. In the left fore-ground, the number 1054 is nothing special, but the car to the right has number 3, first issued in 1903 to a famous Torontonian, Dr. Perry Doolittle, a driving force behind the formation of the Ontario Motor League in 1907 and the Canadian Automobile Association in 1913. The good doctor is very likely the man behind the wheel.

A Spin in High Park

This 1902 Northern automobile with tiller steering and squeeze horn is rolling through High Park in 1906. Licence plates were now made of rubber and cost $4. The licence number seen here, 562, also appears on one of the cowl lamps in compliance with a 1903 Ontario law that stated this number "must be painted in black figures not less than two inches in height on the illuminated glass of a lamp to be carried prominently in the front of the automobile, the glass being ground or stippled with white paint."

The Northern was designed and built in Detroit from 1902 to 1909 by Charles Brady King, reportedly the first man to drive a car on the streets of Detroit (March 6, 1896). He worked for Oldsmobile from 1900 to 1902, then started building cars on his own. At this point, Ransom E. Olds threatened him with a lawsuit for violating the terms of his contract with Oldsmobile. To circumvent the impending court action, C. B. King obtained a brevet (patent) to build a car in Sweden, and about a dozen "Nordens" were manufactured in that northern European country, using some parts imported from the United States. R. E. Olds gradually cooled off (rising sales of his curved-dash Olds helped), and the lawsuit was dropped. C. B. King now began building the Northern in Detroit.

The famous "Silent Northern" was introduced in 1904, so called because of its enormous 10-foot-long muffler that extended to the rear of the car and back to the front again. By 1906, the Northern slogan was "Silent, Safe, and Dustless" because of its long twin mufflers, rugged construction, a pneumatic control lever, and fan blades built into the flywheel to draw cool air in through the front and blow dust out the back (the hood was airtight).

The Price Is Right

This motorist is helping himself to some corn in the Ontario countryside in 1911. No wonder farmers hated the automobile! But they got even in more ways than one. Sometimes they flooded part of the road beside their farm, then charged $5 every time they hitched up their horses and pulled a car out of the mud. They also planted field corn (fit only for livestock) about 20 feet in from the edge of their cornfields. Anybody stealing and eating that corn ended up with a bellyache.

The getaway car used here is a Model T Ford, one of over 15 million built between 1908 and 1927. Henry Ford had gone through several letters of the alphabet (A, B, C, F, K, N, R, and S) in building cars since the formation of the Ford Motor Company on June 16, 1903. His financial backers wanted to concentrate on the luxury car market, but Ford dreamed of building a car so simple and in such enormous volume that nearly everyone could afford a Ford. That dream became a reality on October 1, 1908, when the first Model T (a 1909 model) rolled out of his Detroit factory. The touring model sold for $1,150 in Canada, but that price kept falling as volume increased, especially after the adoption of the assembly line in 1913. The Model T shown here ($975 fully equipped) carries 1911 Ontario licence plates, noteworthy for three reasons: these were the first metal plates issued in Ontario, the first annually issued ones, and the first to carry the year of issue.

Outa My Way

Years ago, Lambton was a community on the outskirts of Toronto, where present-day Old Dundas Street crosses the Humber River. The Eaton family built a public road through this area (one of their many acts of philanthropy), and this thoroughfare was regarded as the best road in the Toronto area when this photo was taken in 1912. The horses apparently are not in a panic at the sight of the speeding car, but the buggy on the right has pulled over and stopped to give the car the right-of-way. We can imagine what the buggy driver thinks of these noisy new contraptions, made even noisier by some motorists who used an exhaust cut-out that bypassed the muffler to gain more speed.

See You at the Auto Show

Auto shows were held in Toronto as far back as April 1904, when the Canada Cycle and Motor Company (CCM) staged a display of the cars it handled and built, including the Ivanhoe Electric. The show was repeated in 1905, then was followed the next year by a full-scale showing of all makes. By 1912, auto shows in Toronto were big business, with two rival shows held that year, one in the St. Lawrence Arena and the other in the University Avenue Armouries.

The show at the Armouries literally waved the flag for Great Britain: a giant Union Jack hung from the ceiling, and 6,000 electric lights illuminated the building at night. A crown 15 feet high and 14 feet across was suspended from the building's roof. The value of the cars on display totalled $1 million, with more than 150 different models featured. About half of these were built in the United States, including the American Underslungs shown here (see page 23).

Slippery When Wet

This little electric car nearly plunged to its death when it left the slippery, snow-covered wooden planks of the Glen Road Bridge, mounted the curb, and broke the railing, seen in this 1912 photo by William James. James must have been fascinated by the accident because he took pictures from several angles, including this one from the floor of the Rosedale ravine. The houses in the background of the next photo are on Howard Avenue, because Bloor Street had not yet been extended east from Sherbourne. When Sherbourne Street was extended north from Bloor into Rosedale, the Glen Road Bridge was replaced by a pedestrian bridge, which is still there.

Women motorists in the early days were very fond of electric cars, perhaps because they were clean and quiet, and could be started without strenuous cranking. Several makes were available, including the Baker Electric (which, in 1902, boasted the first seat belts in a car), the Detroit-Electric, the Rauch & Lang, and the Peck Electric ("Keeps Pecking"), built at 66 Jarvis Street in 1912 and 1913. The Peck cost $4,000 and "at a telephone call, we call for – charge – wash – and deliver cars – for which we make the modest charge of $30 per month."

Stuck in the Mud

Standing around and watching the plight of a motorist stuck in the mud was a popular form of entertainment when the photo on the following page was taken of a Russell touring car on Yonge Street near Balliol Street in 1913. The young man on the sidewalk has his hands in his pockets, not exactly the pose of someone ready and eager to help. The man trying to crank the engine to life is, luckily, wearing knee-high rubber boots. No doubt he welcomes the advice coming his way from over the windshield.

The first Russell cars were known as the Model A (see photo in front of City Hall, page 19) and appeared on the market in 1905. They were built by the Canada Cycle & Motor Company (popularly known as CCM), formed in September of 1899 to cash in on the booming bicycle market. But, glutted by over-production, and with bicycle fever cooling off, that market began to drop dramatically over the next two years, prompting CCM to diversify into automobiles. "Tommy" Russell, then a recent honours graduate in political science at the University of Toronto, joined CCM in 1901 and soon became general manager. He supervised the launching of the 1903 Ivanhoe, an electric vehicle produced in small quantities until 1905. By that time, CCM

was convinced its automotive future lay with large gasoline-powered cars, and the result was the 1905 Model A bearing the Russell name. It featured a flywheel with built-in fan blades and a gearshift lever mounted on the steering column (something most other cars did not adopt until decades later). The cars got bigger and bigger, and by 1912 the Russell had earned a solid reputation as Canada's premier luxury car.

It was the first really successful Canadian automobile and the only successful Canadian car to evolve from a bicycle company instead of a carriage builder.

Unfortunately, when this photo was taken in 1913 the entire company was becoming mired in difficulties. Two new models introduced that year developed serious production problems, and output from the West Toronto factory was a mere trickle. These problems persisted into 1914   but

then war broke out in Europe, and the company's attention was diverted to munitions production.

Automobile production continued, but on a reduced scale, and in the fall of 1915 the company received an offer that was too good to refuse. John North Willys had built the Willys-Overland Company in Toledo, Ohio, into the second largest manufacturer of automobiles in the world and was now ready to expand into Canada. He bought the automobile portion of the Russell Company and used the West Toronto factory to build Willys-Overland cars until 1928. Production of the Russell car ended forever in December 1915.

But Tommy Russell still had a quarter of a century to go. He served as president of CCM for many years, then as president of the Massey-Harris Company from 1930 until his death on December 29, 1940. One of the cars bearing his name showed up on a used car lot in Montreal in the early 1950s. It was a 1914 four-cylinder Russell Knight (serial number 969), featuring the famous "Silent Knight" sleeve-valve engine available in Russell cars since 1910. The Montreal Russell passed through the hands of several collectors over the years, then became part of an estate sale in 1990. Mike Filey featured the car in his "The Way We Were" column in the *Toronto Sun* on June 29, 1990 ("Auto Heritage May Hit the Road"): "The asking price is $29,000. Early inquiries indicate that the Toronto-built piece of Canadian transportation history may soon be on its way to Belgium. Any guardian angels of Canadian history out there?"

Filey's question was answered in a way no one could have imagined. Mike himself tells it best in his book, *Toronto Sketches* (published in 1992 by Dundurn Press): "Two days after (my) article appeared, I received a call from Tommy

Russell's daughter who wanted to know who she might speak with to learn more about the car. I gave her what details I had and she indicated that she would definitely call me back to report any progress in keeping the car in Canada.

As it turned out, not only did she buy the car, but she is also having it restored to 1914 condition. Thanks, Betty."

Betty's father, Tommy Russell, is seated behind the wheel, far left, at City Hall, 1905.

Auto Polo at the CNE

"Automobiles appeared in a sports event at the (CNE) grand-stand... in 1913, and before a capacity crowd, the hair-raising capabilities of the vehicles were displayed, in the form of auto-polo. For this game, the cars were stripped to the chassis, leaving two seats over the gas tank, one for the driver, and the other for the mallet man. The driver skilfully twisted and turned the car, sometimes upside-down, as he endeavoured to get close enough to the ball, for the mallet man, standing on the running board, to hit it toward the opponent's goal. It was a tremendously exciting sport."

from *Once Upon a Century: 100 Year History of the 'Ex'*

You Can Drive But You Can't Vote

This Model T Ford roadster is parked in front of a medical facility at 386 King Street West. The year is probably 1914. The nurse standing beside the car could drive it, but did not have the right to vote. Manitoba became the first province to grant women this right, on January 27, 1916. Saskatchewan followed about two months later, and Alberta a few weeks after that. Ontario women joined their ranks on April 12, 1917. Winning the right to vote in federal elections took longer. Robert Borden's Conservative government passed the Wartime Elections Act in 1917 to gather support for its policy of conscription. This act gave the vote to wives, widows, mothers, sisters, and daughters of Canadian soldiers serving overseas. When the war reached its final year, Canadian men finally recognized the outstanding contribution to the war effort made by Canadian women such as the one pictured here. Their struggle for the right to vote achieved total victory by May 24, 1918.

Wartime Jitney

During the First World War, the CNE grounds were used as an army camp. Serving the local travel needs of the soldiers was this Model T Ford touring car, one of 104 jitneys or "dime buses" available for hire, just like a taxi but usually following a regular route with a flexible schedule. The word jitney, used as early as 1903, was a slang term for nickel and came to be applied to small buses with a 5-cent fare. The fare had doubled by 1914, which goes to show inflation is nothing new.

The Tanks Are Coming

A tank crushes a car on University Avenue around 1917 to stimulate recruitment, the scrap metal drive, and the sale of Victory bonds. In 1915, the British had built the first armour-plated motorized vehicles with caterpillar treads for crossing trenches, and they were first used in the Battle of the Somme in 1916. Winston Churchill was an early and eager advocate of these new vehicles and secretly diverted funds from his own war department for their development because the British top brass thought the whole idea would be a waste of money. And why do we call them tanks? The first of these vehicles were shipped to France in large crates labelled TANK to deceive the German spies into thinking they were water tanks. The name stuck.

Your Country Needs You

Toronto Mayor Tommy Church is wearing a straw hat at this recruitment rally in front of the City Hall in 1916. Next to him is Reverend J. D. Morrow, while J. W. Geddes stands on the front seat of this sporty roadster and urges all able-bodied civilians to enlist in the war effort. By this time, the war had been grinding on for two long years with no end in sight. The slaughter on the battlefields of Europe would ultimately cost the lives of 60,000 Canadians — and those who were slow to volunteer were the target of undisguised hostility. A billboard on University Avenue showed a young girl asking her father: "And what did you do in the Great War, Daddy?" Less subtle were public tauntings and back-alley beatings. By 1917, the shortage of manpower in the

trenches triggered the conscription crisis, which left behind a residue of bitterness that lasted far longer than the war itself.

The American Underslung shown here was the brain-child of Harry Stutz (of Stutz Bearcat fame). The Under-slung was built in Indianapolis from 1905 to 1914 and derived its name and low profile from the design of the frame, mounted below the axle. A great car for those who had the money to buy it and the time to drive it.

Armistice Day
Hood Ornament

The "war to end all wars" finally came to an end on November 11, 1918. Toronto went wild as people danced in the streets, with music supplied by pianos hoisted onto the roofs of streetcars. The noise of celebration was deafening – and this curly-haired young girl with the high-button boots welcomed the first day of peace while perched on the hood of a Model T Ford. The Ford script on the radiator was first used in 1903 (the year the company was formed) and is still in use today.

PART TWO

Between the Wars, 1918-1939

The opening of the Prince Edward Viaduct just before the end of the First World War gave Toronto motorists easy access to the lands east of the Don Valley and literally paved the way for rapid urban growth on either side of Danforth Avenue. Toronto also spread out to the north and west all through the 1920s, and wherever new roads were built, cars were there to use them. Not even the Depression could dampen Toronto's love affair with the automobile. If you couldn't afford a new car in the 1930s, you could find a used car in running condition to fit almost any budget. In 1934, one man acquired a 1922 Model T Ford in exchange for a screen door off the back of the house he and his family were to be evicted from the next day (see page 83).

Meanwhile, the new cars got bigger, faster and more streamlined. When the King and Queen visited Canada in the spring of 1939, they officially dedicated a new concrete superhighway of the future between Toronto and Niagara Falls: the Queen Elizabeth Way. Toronto's cars and roads had come a long way since 1918.

A Growing
Danforth Business

In 1927, Canada was sixty years old and the country celebrated its Diamond Jubilee. From coast to coast, communities large and small fanned the flames of civic pride by extolling the achievements of their residents. The following article, condensed from an official souvenir program of the Canadian Diamond Jubilee, tells the story of a well-known Toronto car dealer:

"Some men must wander far from their birthplaces to achieve outstanding success in life. Not so Bill Giles. He was born in Scarboro' township – December 11, 1892 – and all his life has been spent within a radius of four and a half miles of his birthplace. He did not even go into 'downtown'

Toronto to seek his fortune; he pinned his faith on the Danforth district. That faith, coupled with plenty of hard work, brought him a tremendous business as the Danforth grew up. Educated at Scarboro' township public school No. 8, Mr Giles started in business for himself the year he attained his majority. His first venture was a wholesale milk business, but when the Chevrolet motor car entered Canada in 1915 he foresaw the future of this growing mode of transportation and obtained the Chevrolet franchise for Scarboro'. That first year, in spite of the newness of his product and his own inexperience, he sold five cars. The business grew until he was forced to expand, and the present firm of Giles, Rice and Peters was formed in 1919.

"When the sensational new Pontiac was introduced in 1926, Mr Giles at once saw the opportunity offered by this low-priced high-quality six cylinder automobile. He immediately organized the firm of W. S. Giles Limited to handle the new line. Although only a year old, this new firm already bids fair to rival the success of its sister business situated at 348 Danforth Avenue, a considerable distance west of the other. W. S. Giles Limited has sold a surprising number of Pontiacs."

The above photo, taken in 1931, shows the Giles, Rice and Peters Ltd. tow truck in use at that time. The business at 348 Danforth was taken over in October 1928 by an early sales manager, George Hogan, who operated Hogan Pontiac Buick Co. Ltd. until the early 1980s. In the 1970s, the dealership boasted a sales staff who could speak a total of twenty languages among them, reflecting the growing cultural diversity of Toronto's east end.

Mount Pleasant Mud

This Model T Ford commercial vehicle is rolling through the mud on Mount Pleasant Road around 1920. The passenger side of the hood is folded open, perhaps to alleviate an overheating problem. The tombstones in the background belong to Mount Pleasant Cemetery, which had its first interment on March 13, 1876, when the city of Toronto had a population of 68,000 people.

Stretching from Yonge Street to Bayview Avenue and covering a total of 200 acres, the cemetery originally had no thoroughfare through the middle of it. By the time the city of Toronto annexed the town of North Toronto in 1912, two unpaved and unconnected streets called Mount Pleasant Road (named after the cemetery) ran north and south of the cemetery and (if you'll pardon the terminology) dead-ended at the edge of the property. Pressure began mounting for a direct link between north and south to aid the rapidly growing volume of vehicular traffic between uptown and downtown. Work began on the link in 1917, and it opened for traffic in 1919. The mud remained until 1925, when Mount Pleasant Road was paved between St. Clair and Eglinton avenues.

Get Your New Chevy Here

This photo, taken November 22, 1921, shows a Chevrolet
dealer at 2574 Yonge Street, near Albertus Avenue, in a building
occupied today by a clothing store. Chevrolet at that time still
had a long way to go to surpass the Model T Ford in sales. It
finally did so in 1927, and its success contributed greatly to
Henry Ford's decision to end the Model T and bring out the
Model A. It is interesting to note that the car parked in front of
the garage is a Model T Ford. Perhaps a customer's car being
traded in? Perhaps the photographer's car? Or maybe
the sales manager's car! Also note the wooden sidewalk
in front and the single track of the radial railway that
ran up the west side of Yonge Street at that time.

The Canadian Tire Story

The Canadian Tire Corporation can trace its roots back to
the Hamilton Tire & Garage Ltd., a Ford dealer at the
corner of Gerrard and Hamilton streets just west of Broad-
view Avenue in Riverdale. It opened for business in 1909
and specialized in buying surplus tires from manufacturers
in the winter (when most motorists put their cars up on
blocks) and selling them at discount prices in the summer.

Seventeen-year-old Bill Billes was hired on as sales manager in 1913. Opportunity knocked in 1922 when the owners
of the Hamilton Tire & Garage Ltd. offered to sell their
business to Bill for $1,800. He invited his younger brother
Alf to join him and, on September 15 of that year, the Billes
brothers went into business. "Our money was being made on
cars," Alf later recalled. "In those days cars weren't very
good. You always had trouble starting them. So, if you had
money, you parked it in a heated garage. [Parking cars] was
how I learned to drive."

The following year they closed down and reopened at
Yonge and Gould; soon after that they moved into a retail
outlet at 639 Yonge Street at Isabella, on the edge of downtown Toronto. The city by this time had 40,000 cars, and the
business prospered with sales of tires, toolboxes, batteries,
windshield wipers, car heaters, automatic starters, and a
homemade anti-freeze that Alf mixed in the basement.

The big money-maker in the early years was tires, and a

motorist was lucky to get a thousand miles out of them. Some drivers put milk and molasses in them to try and strengthen them – but what an awful stench when the tire blew! Complaints of tire failure were a constant hassle at the store, so the Billes brothers solved this problem by offering an unconditional one-year guarantee. The tires were still as unreliable as ever, but the publicity generated by the guarantee brought in lots of extra business.

To handle the expansion, the brothers moved across Isabella to 637 Yonge Street in 1927 and changed their name to Canadian Tire Corporation Limited. "We used Canadian Tire because it sounded big," Alf said, and with the mail-order side of the business steadily growing, the firm was soon on its way to living up to its new name.

The final move came in 1937 when the brothers moved their main store and headquarters to an abandoned supermarket at 827–847 Yonge Street, just north of Yonge and Davenport in mid-town Toronto.

The main store is still there today. This 1959 photograph shows the south end of the store and the Canadian Tire gas station on the corner. A 1956 Meteor waits in the chill winter air as a '58 Pontiac gasses up at the pumps. In the background is the large neon sign for the Austin dealership next door, not yet forced out of business by German and Japanese imports. The Austin property is now a Canadian Tire parking lot.

The Mills and Hadwin Story

These new cars are lined up in front of Mills and Hadwin in 1929. Note the letter "C" has fallen off the building from Waverley Garage Co. The billboard would be worth its weight in gold at a flea market today. But the story began in 1919, when Joe Mills came out of the Air Force and began repairing cars as a roving mechanic. In 1922, he decided he wanted a garage of his own. He purchased the lot on Yonge Street where Mills and Hadwin is now located and began construction of a building which is still in use today. But before the building progressed beyond the footings stage, Joe Mills took sick and died.

Joe's brother Guy came to the rescue, and the building was finally completed by Labour Day, 1922. It had a tar-paper roof and an inadequate heating system; the repair shop was heated by a station agent's stove, and a jacket heater in the basement was connected to the single rad in the showroom.

North Yonge Street was a risky place to go into the car business in the early 1920s. The street had only a rough macadam surface, with mostly open land on either side, an occasional house, and three or four stores to the north. Lawrence Park, to the south, was only partially built. There were no sewers and no electricity, and the only public transportation was a single-track radial railway running up the west side of Yonge. Side streets were a nightmare of mud in the spring and dirt and dust in the summer. Only the main roads were ploughed in the winter. One day, soon after opening for business, Guy Mills was waiting his turn in the neighbourhood barbershop. The barber and his customer in the chair were discussing the new garage down the street. "They won't last long," the barber remarked. We'll see about that, thought Guy.

But he faced a tough job. He had no experience whatsoever in the car sales or repair business (he had been managing a correspondence school downtown when his brother Joe died).

To overcome this handicap, Guy persuaded Lou Hadwin to join him. Hadwin had been managing a small General Motors dealership down Yonge Street and brought with him a wealth of experience. Thus Mills and Hadwin was born.

In 1923, opportunity knocked in the form of the Star, a new car that the Durant Motor Company had introduced the previous year. It had many advanced features for that time, including a disk clutch, a water pump, an oil pump, and spiral bevel gears in the rear end. It was designed to compete head-on with the Model T Ford, but was mechanically superior.

The Canadian factory for Durant Motors was located on Laird Drive in Leaside. (The building, now empty, is still standing, on the same property as Canada Wire and Cable.)

Mills and Hadwin began selling the Star, as well as the Durant and Flint, and these sales helped the business to earn modest profits through the 1920s. But selling cars was not always easy back then. Credit arrangements were difficult and the manufacturer had to be paid cash on delivery. This meant you often had to sell the customer's trade-in before you could deliver the new car. And this often required having access to the trade-in while the car was still in use.

Many first-time car buyers did not know how to drive, and Mills and Hadwin had to provide driving lessons to close the deal. To complicate matters, early transmissions had no

Cutting the ribbon to open the gas station. Note clear-vision gas pumps. Sign says: "Be here 7 p.m. Friday, June 7. First 50 customers get 2 gallons free."

synchromesh and drivers had to learn how to double-clutch while shifting gears.

In 1928, Mills and Hadwin were able to purchase an additional 75 feet of frontage on the south side of their property and persuaded the British and American Oil Company to build a service station there. It opened at 7 p.m. on Friday, June 7, 1929, with a big sign in front: "First 50 Customers Get 2 Gallons Free."

Car sales fell sharply after the stock market crash in October of 1929, and one car company after another was forced out of business. Durant Motors in the United States had gone heavily into debt to build its 1930 models, using as collateral its controlling interest in Durant Motors of

Publicity photo of 1927 Star
rumble-seat roadster, typical of the new cars
sold by Mills and Hadwin over sixty years ago.

Canada. When the U.S. firm defaulted on the loan, its Canadian subsidiary re-organized itself as an independent company known as Dominion Motors, on March 14, 1931. The factory was soon turning out a distinctly Canadian car patterned after the Durant and known as the Frontenac. But this car too became a casualty of hard times, despite valiant efforts to promote it, including sales people across the country dressed in the garb, wig, and goatee of Count Frontenac, seventeenth-century governor of New France. Production came to an end in 1933. That's the year Mills and Hadwin

began selling Plymouths and Chryslers, and they have done so ever since.

In 1952, after thirty years in the business, Lou Hadwin died, and his loss was keenly felt. In 1979, Guy Mills, then nearly ninety, decided it was time to sell the business (he died seven years later, in 1986). The new owner and president, Jack Philips, had joined Mills and Hadwin in 1946 and served for years as a self-confessed "bean counter," keeping a watchful eye on the balance between expenses and income. His timely purchase of the business in 1979 demonstrated his faith in the future not only of Mills and Hadwin but of the Chrysler Corporation itself.

The North Yonge dealership is still going strong after more than seventy years. And what is the secret behind this amazing success? It was summed up in three words in a 1972 article celebrating Mills and Hadwin's first half-century of service: "Treat people right."

Car Meets Streetcar

During the 1920s, the Ontario Safety League staged a number of "accidents" between cars and streetcars to encourage motorists to use extra caution when driving in the vicinity of TTC vehicles. This 1923 photo looks north along a tree-lined Avenue Road a couple of blocks north of Bloor Street. British and American Motors is open for business across the street at 99 Avenue Road, on the site now occupied by Hazelton Lanes. Your 1923 dollars could buy a McLaughlin (a Canadian Buick), a GMC truck, or – if you wanted to really splurge – a Marmon, a luxury car built in Indianapolis from 1902 to 1933. The first Indianapolis 500 race was won by the Marmon Wasp 6-cylinder racer in 1911. It carried one of the first rearview mirrors ever used on a car. Because the Marmon was built in limited numbers and carried a hefty price tag, it was often sold through dealerships that offered more mundane automobiles. This arrangement gave Marmon more sales outlets and gave the dealership the opportunity to score a fat profit on each one sold. British and American Motors had also handled a large and luxurious English car, the Wolseley, from 1912 to 1920. Just a short distance south of this location is a popular modern-day Toronto attraction: the McLaughlin Planetarium, named after its benefactor, Col. Sam McLaughlin (1871–1972), who served for many years as president of General Motors of Canada.

Christmas Eve 1924

With Santa Claus due to hit town in a few hours, Toronto motorists start heading for home on this final day of Christmas shopping. This Bay Street photo looking north was taken at Temperance Street, with the General Assurance Building on the right, on the site of the carriage factory that built Toronto's first car in 1893 (see page 4). The Kiwanis International sign can be seen just above "A Merry Xmas" on the City Hall in the background. You can tell by the snow (or lack of it) on the roofs of cars which ones were parked outside during the last snowfall. Some motorists covered their hoods with blankets to keep the engine warm, and probably got the idea from a horse like the one on the left.

Repairs to All Makes

The Agincourt Garage stood for years at the southwest corner of Victoria Park and Sheppard avenues. This photo from the 1920s shows the Ontario Motor League tow truck operated by J. W. Kennedy and Son, who made "repairs to all makes." They could be reached by ringing up the operator at "24, please" during the day, or "26, please" after dark. The clear-vision gas pumps enabled motorists to see they were getting clean gasoline. The pumps shown here had the number of gallons clearly marked on the glass to assure the motorist of an accurate quantity and price.

The word "gasoline" appeared in print as early as 1865 to describe a dangerous and useless byproduct of the oil refining business. It was dumped on the ground, burned, or simply thrown away because nobody had a use for it — until the 1890s and the arrival of gasoline-powered horseless carriages.

Model T at Bala, 1925

A ten-year-old Model T Ford touring car, dubbed "HENRY XV," looks ready for action in a parking lot in Bala in 1925. A perfect car for running out of gas on the back roads of Muskoka! The removal of front fenders was a common practice among young people anxious to make their car look like a jalopy. "Children cry for it" was a slogan used for years by Fletcher's Castoria.

You Fix the Car, I'll Fix My Face

It's springtime 1926 and the blossoms are in bloom near Grimsby, Ontario. If you look closely, you can see the vase full of flowers mounted on the inside of the door post behind the driver's door. John and Edna Boyd of Toronto are the busy couple in this candid shot (or was it posed?). Note the Toronto nameplate below the licence plate, a badge of civic pride in bygone years.

Free Auto Laundry

These cars are taking a bath in the Humber River near Dundas Street on July 16, 1927. But they are not there just to get the dust and dirt off. Many of these cars have wooden spoke wheels which dry out with age, causing the spokes to shrink and the wheels to wobble. If the car is parked for a while in a river, the wooden spikes swell up, making the wheels as good as new again.

Going Back to the Horse

This woman is making good use of the running board on this one-year-old 1927 LaSalle, a car introduced by General Motors in March of that year as a less expensive "companion" car to the Cadillac. The LaSalle insignia on the crossbar between the headlights was a distinctive styling feature for many years. The wing nuts on either side of the windshield could be loosened to fold the windshield flat above the hood for a wind-in-the-face driving thrill (not unlike the wind in your face when you're riding a horse). Also note the crank hole cover, the exposed horn, the cowl lights, the single windshield wiper, and the louvers in the side of the hood, all common features on cars of that time. The LaSalle was terminated by General Motors after the 1940-model year (see page 68).

Stuck in the Tracks on Yonge Street

Looking north on Yonge Street near Carlton around 1928. The car stuck between the tracks is a 1904 Ford, one of the first models of Ford to be built in Canada. Painted on the side of the car is the name "See and Duggan," a Ford dealer for many years on the east side of Yonge just a few blocks north of where this picture was taken. The car, already a quarter-century old, was perhaps being driven to a dealer-sponsored publicity event when this mishap occurred.

Stop!

This Toronto police officer is mounting a brake-testing device on the running board of a car on March 28, 1929. He then steps up onto the running board, wraps his arm around the door post, and tells the driver to take the car up to 20 miles per hour. Once that speed is reached, the driver slams on the brakes and brings the car to a halt. Some cars stopped so fast that the officer was thrown forward against the front fender. The device on the running board gave the brakes a numerical rating that indicated whether or not they were safe.

Many cars back then had two-wheel brakes, and those that had four-wheel brakes carried a metal triangle mounted on the left rear fender warning other drivers not to follow too closely. The first road test of four-wheel brakes in Toronto took place in 1913 on King Street West near the Royal Alex when the driver of a Toronto-built Bartlett automobile slammed on the brakes. Twenty-six cars smashed into each other behind him, giving Toronto its worst multi-vehicle accident up to that time. Maybe those cars should have been equipped with a device available on the Toronto-built Jules car in 1911: a horn button mounted in the middle of the brake pedal.

Traffic at Queen and Yonge, 1929

Shoppers and gawkers thronged the sidewalks during the noon hour at Queen and Yonge on August 31, 1929, little knowing the bottom would fall out of the stock market in another two months. The roadster with its top down at the intersection is heading north and followed closely by what appears to be a Model T Ford centre-door sedan. The Heintzman Piano building in the background is still there today, as is the old Bank of Montreal building on the northeast corner. Then, as now, the streets were crowded with cars.

CNE Car Crash, circa 1930

If you have ever wondered where all the old cars have gone, here's what happened to two of them at the CNE grandstand around 1930. "Wreck 'em" races and demolition derbies were part of the Toronto automotive scene well into the 1950s, and hundreds of old jalopies ended their lives with a CRASH! BANG! CRUNCH! WHEEZE! THUD! in front of thousands of screaming spectators. What a way to go!

Here's the Beef

Traffic was blocked in the St. Clair-Keele area when this cow escaped from a Swift's Premium slaughterhouse around 1930. The car is a 1929 Oldsmobile F-29 convertible roadster with landau bars, a fold-down windshield, and suicide doors with crank-up windows. The small key-locked door just ahead of the rear fender provides access to the golf club compartment, and the handle behind the roof opens the rumble seat. This car was powered by a 197-cubic-inch L-head 6-cylinder engine first introduced the previous year. In fact, all 1929 Oldsmobiles (all 94,598 of them in all body styles, of which the one shown here was rare) were slightly modified versions of the all-new 1928 Oldsmobile F-28, a car thoroughly road-tested by the worst drivers General Motors could find. The result was a very rugged and durable automobile.

Pierce-Arrow Showroom

The CBC building that stands today at 1140 Yonge Street was once home to some of the most magnificent automobiles ever sold in Toronto. H. E. Givan Ltd. opened for business on Monday, January 13, 1930, as the flagship Toronto dealership of the prestigious Pierce-Arrow, a luxury motor car built in Buffalo, New York, from 1901 to 1938. Its 1930 prices ranged as high as $9,450 at a time when a new Model A Ford sold for $540.

Constructed on the site of a former Methodist church, the new brick, stone, and concrete building was highlighted by ten large, arched showroom windows. Seven of these faced Yonge Street, and the middle one served as the showroom entrance, flanked by two ornate lights under an outstretched Pierce-Arrow sign. Two other arches faced Marlborough Street to the north, and the final arch was placed diagonally across the corner to display cars for the benefit of south-bound Yonge Street traffic. This arch serves today as the entrance to the building.

The showroom inside those arched windows had plenty of floor space to display the new cars, thanks to a mezzanine level that housed the company's offices. The new cars included Studebakers as well as Pierce-Arrows because the two companies were joined together from 1928 to 1933. A large used car showroom and service bay occupied the rear of the building, and one of the old grease pits is still there under a new floor.

Opening day at the new dealership was trumpeted by a half-page ad in *The Globe*, claiming that the "new showrooms are the most beautiful in Toronto." All this happened less than three months after the big stock market crash of 1929.

As the Depression deepened, car sales dropped lower and lower, and plans to add an extra two storeys above the service bay were cancelled. By 1937, production at the Pierce-Arrow factory had fallen to about seventeen cars, and the remaining assets of the company were auctioned off the following year.

H. E. Givan Ltd. was able to remain at 1140 Yonge Street for another three years by selling other car makes, then moved to another location, further south on Yonge in 1941. In the building they left behind, armament shells were made on three shifts a day during the Second World War. Other uses over the years included the selling of Grew boats and the marketing of RCA Victor radios.

Finally, in 1954, the CBC moved into the building. On September 25, 1978, the building was listed as historical by the City of Toronto, thereby helping to preserve its faded glory for future generations.

The Copps of Don Mills pose here with their Pierce-Arrow in 1939.

Where Are They Now?

At least one Pierce-Arrow that was sold new from the showroom at 1140 Yonge Street still exists: a straight-eight, 137-inch-wheelbase 1932 Model 54 convertible coupe. It was assembled at the Studebaker factory in Walkerville, Ontario (now part of the city of Windsor), with parts manufactured in Buffalo, New York. The car was bought new in 1933 by Lady Kerr of Willowdale, who sold or traded it with unknown mileage in 1936 to Hogan Pontiac Ltd. in Toronto. The second owner, A. W. Copp of Don Mills, bought it from Hogan's for $600 with a 1928 Willys-Knight trade-in, and kept it for the next fourteen years. During that time, the

A Pierce-Arrow roadster is shown at the Eglinton Hunt Club on Avenue Road around 1929. Very probably, these four heavily-clad folks squeezed into the front seat for the ride home because the rumble seat was no place to be in the dead of winter. The fender-mounted head-lights had been a Pierce-Arrow trademark since 1913 and were finally adopted by the rest of the industry in the 1930s. A Toronto man named Earl Domm worked in the paint department of the Pierce-Arrow factory in Buffalo in the late 1920s and his office was beside the place where the body men hammer-welded the headlight housings onto the fenders. Mr. Domm, now ninety, says he can still hear the banging of those hammers from over sixty years ago.

original front bumper was broken and replaced with a truck unit, the running boards were replaced with heavy steel plate, a non-factory heater was installed, and the car was repainted turquoise.

The car was sold again in 1950, to a used car lot affiliated with Gorries Chev-Olds, for $350, with approximately 65,000 miles on the odometer. John Anderson of Toronto then pur-chased it for $525 from Belmont Motors on Danforth Avenue — and still owns the car! During the last forty-odd years, the car has been reupholstered and a new con- vertible top fabri-cated and installed. The engine has been rebuilt and the bright-work replated. The car now awaits restoration of the body and a return to its 1932 showroom condition.

Two Packards in Ontario Since New

Bruce Cole of Ancaster, Ontario, is the proud owner of a 1931 Packard convertible sedan he purchased in 1954. Bert Campbell owns one almost identical to it. Bruce writes:

"In the early summer of 1931, Ontario Packard Company of Toronto had two new model 833 convertible sedans in their showrooms for sale. These would be the first factory built bodies of this style available. Before 1931, if you wanted a convertible sedan, it would require a special order from one of the custom coach builders at extra cost to the buyer.

"These two Packards were almost identical except for colour, and the fact the blue car had the Standard Eight ribbed hood while the brown and beige car came with the three doors on the side of the hood. Both cars were delivered with real leather upholstery, dark blue in one and rich brown in the other.

"Although both cars were Packard's middle priced models ($3,600.00), they were loaded with most of Packard's deluxe accessories, with the best of chrome plating. Nineteen-thirty-one was a tough year to be selling luxury automobiles and all these extras were added to the deal to bring about a successful sale.

"I don't know who the first owners were, but both cars have been in Ontario all of their time."

Three Years Old in '32

George Bernard of Toronto purchased a new Plymouth road-ster with rumble seat in 1929, the same year in which his wife, Monica, presented him with a brand-new baby boy named Julian. Three years later, in July of 1932, that same Plymouth roadster carried George and his young family to a picnic spot outside Toronto, where this picture was taken. Monica is behind the wheel but did not drive the car that day. In fact, she drove it only once, and when she did, it went off the road and hit a tree — with no damage to anything except Monica's desire to keep driving. The little boy clutch-ing his teddy bear behind the car is Julian, and the occasion is his third birthday (Julian, now retired, still lives in Toronto and is an active member of the North Toronto Historical Society). Soon after the photo was taken, Julian's younger brother was born, and George Bernard traded the Plymouth for a large 1928 Hudson four-door sedan to pro-vide more room for his growing family.

A Packard Fit
for a King

Holding a pair of gloves in his right hand, Frank "King" Clancy poses with pride alongside his 1932 Packard Series 900 Light Eight "shovelnose" coupe on March 17, 1933. Clancy made a name for himself as a hockey player in Ottawa, then was lured to Toronto when Conn Smythe traded two players and $35,000 to get him. He was paired with Hap Day on defence, and the Maple Leafs won the Stanley Cup the following year (1931), which was also their first season in the newly constructed Maple Leaf Gardens at the northwest corner of Church and Carlton, acclaimed at the time as the best arena in the world.

For millions of hockey fans, "King" Clancy became a household name, thanks in part to the radio voice of Foster "He shoots! He scores!" Hewitt. For decades, Clancy was associated with the Toronto Maple Leafs as coach and general manager of the National Hockey League club.

His choice of car was an interesting one. Like most other car companies, Packard was reeling under the impact of the Depression when it introduced the Light Eight in January of 1932. It was designed to tap into the upper-medium-priced market and to entice buyers away from the larger Buicks, Chryslers, Nashes, and Studebakers. It was available in four body styles: a four-door sedan ($1,750 US), a two-door sedan, a stationary coupe with a padded roof, and an open version known as the "coupe roadster" (these latter three were priced at $1,795 US). The Light Eight had modern styling, Packard quality, good performance, and good handling, with the 110-horsepower, straight-eight engine mounted slightly aft of the front wheels to make the steering easier (an attractive feature for Packard owners who could no longer afford a chauffeur).

The new Light Eight had everything in its favour –

except its ability to earn a profit. It was priced hundreds of dollars below the Packard Standard Eight ($2,650), yet it cost almost as much to produce. In mid-year, the price of the Light Eight was jacked up another $145 in a frantic attempt to halt the rising tide of red ink. And to make matters worse, the ones the company did sell pulled sales away from the more expensive (and more profitable) senior Packards. By the end of 1932, Packard sales had dropped a staggering 81 percent and the company had lost nearly $7 million that year. Just over 9,000 Packards of all kinds were sold in 1932, and about 6,600 of those were the non-profit Light Eights. By January of 1933, the Light Eight was gone.

Although it resembles a convertible, "King" Clancy's Packard is probably the stationary coupe, judging by the padded look of the roof and the large rear window. The ultimate fate of this car is unknown.

At least one Packard Light Eight "coupe roadster" was sold new in Toronto in 1932. It was still around in 1955 when Steve Premock Sr. bought the car from a man in Simcoe, Ontario, for (are you ready for this?) $25 and then stored it indoors for many years at his wrecking yard in Waterford, Ontario. In the 1980s, Steve and his son (Steve Jr.) restored the car to its original showroom condition. The car remains in the Premock family to this day.

Steve Premock Sr. stands proudly beside his $25 Packard after completion of restoration in 1991. The nameplate on the car indicates it was built in Windsor, Ontario, and was delivered to the Toronto dealership of Packard Ontario Motor Company Ltd. on "11-10-32." It is believed to be the only Canadian-built Packard of its kind still in existence.

Smiling in the Depression

Running boards proved their worth over and over again as people posed for the camera between the front and rear fenders. This Toronto lass adorns the driver's side of a 1933 Graham four-door sedan owned by the manager of the downtown office of the Liquor Control Board of Ontario. Note the skirted fender, introduced on the 1932 Graham Blue Streak Eight and adopted industry-wide in North America by the mid-1930s. Note also the crank-out windshield, a popular feature in the days before air conditioning. The Graham name first appeared on the Graham-Paige when the three Graham brothers took over the Paige automobile company in Detroit in 1928. The Paige name was dropped after 1930, and the Graham Hollywood of 1940/41 (built with Cord 810/812 dies and a Hupmobile chassis) marked the end of the brothers' name on an automobile. Train Motors on Yonge Street acted as the Toronto distributor, but very few, if any, Graham Hollywoods were sold in wartime Canada.

Get a Horse!

Stuck in the mud between Bloor Street and
Lakeshore Road around 1934, Art Wells (in fedora on
left) was driving this *Toronto Daily Star* staff car when
his rear wheels became mired in the muck. In spite of
all that horsepower under his hood (at least 50), a pair
of real horses had to be hitched up to haul him out.

Rolling Through the Adirondacks

This brand-new Dodge two-door sedan is whizzing through
the Adirondack Mountains in upper New York State in the
summer of 1934 with its proud new owner behind the wheel:
Miss Baird of Albertus Avenue in Toronto.

The car came from the factory with a three-spoke steering wheel in the shape of an inverted Y. Because Miss Baird
was so short, she had to look through the steering wheel to
drive. The top spoke blocked her line of vision, so the dealer
took the wheel off and mounted it upside-down. Now Miss
Baird was ready for the road.

Her car was equipped with "free-wheeling," a popular
feature in the early thirties that disengaged the clutch every
time you took your foot off the gas. Your car then coasted
down the highway without the benefit of engine braking.
Miss Baird thought this was wonderful until shortly after
this picture was taken. She was rolling down a steep hill
when the brakes failed. She sailed through a busy intersection, narrowly missing other cars, and came to a stop at a gas
station halfway up the hill on the other side. She ordered the
attendant to disconnect that blankety-blank free wheeling
at once.

He did as he was told, but he left the free-wheeling unit mounted under the hood. That's where it stayed for the next thirty-odd years, until Miss Baird finally sold the car. Toronto high-school teacher Ron Hill bought it and treated the car to a body-off restoration. The easiest part of the car to restore was the free-wheeling unit, still as fresh and new as the day it was disconnected in 1934.

This Dodge, incidentally, has a couple of features of interest to radio buffs. To install an original radio in this car, the ash tray must be removed from the dashboard to make room for the radio controls. In other words, you have to choose between smoking and listening to the radio. The fabric insert on the roof is embedded with chicken wire that serves as an antenna. No whip aerials for this old buggy!

Picnic in the Bush

While Miss Baird was testing her free-wheeling in the Adirondacks, other Toronto motorists were lured up north on gravel roads to savour the natural beauty and splendour of Algonquin Park. These hardy fellows reached their picnic spot in a '28-'29 Model A Ford coach and a Buick four-door sedan of similar vintage. The windshield on the Buick has been cranked up a few inches to provide a primitive but environmentally friendly form of air conditioning.

University and Queen, circa 1934

Looking south along University Avenue from just north of Queen Street around 1934. The northbound lanes of University north of Queen were under construction, forcing northbound traffic to use some of the southbound lanes. The big Ford V-8 sign ("Watch the Fords go by") on the roof of the building in the background advertised Henry Ford's latest engineering marvel: the first V-8 engine in the low-priced field. It was introduced in March of 1932 after Ford spent $300 million on its development. The engine block had to be cast in a single piece (which many thought impossible) to keep production costs down, and it remained in production, with some modifications, for nearly a quarter of a century. The roadster in the left foreground is a 1932 Ford Model B with a 4-cylinder engine, a carryover from the Model A. From 1932 until 1934, Ford offered you a choice between a four and a V-8, until all the fours were used up. The roadster seen here is clearly a Model B because it has no V-8 emblem on the crossbar between the headlights.

Gord Hazlett: Old-Time Storyteller

Born August 19, 1919, Gord Hazlett grew up on Ashdale Avenue in Toronto's east end. Because of the Depression, he left school on a work permit at age fourteen and began his apprenticeship as an auto mechanic at Elliot's Garage in the Queen-Greenwood area around 1934. Fifty years later, Gord retired, after half a century of repairing cars and trucks at twenty-three different places around the city. He lives with his wife, Lorraine, of fifty-three years (they have five children and seven grandchildren) in a house Gord built himself on an East York lot purchased by his father in 1924. Making good use of his retirement, Gord drives to cruise nights and flea markets all through the motoring season in his low mileage 1927 Pontiac landau sedan, a car he has owned for thirty-five years. An active member of three antique car clubs, Gord writes hilarious nostalgic articles every two weeks for *Old Autos,* a cross-Canada newspaper. The story of Gord's first car is reprinted here:

"Once upon a time, actually the spring of 1936, a sixteen-year-old kid, actually it was me, bought a dream car, actually it was nearly a whole 1923 'T' model coupe, and spent every cent he had, actually it was $10.00 spot cash, so he could be a member of the motoring public. The car was bought from Ivan's Trailers on Eastern Avenue in the east end of Toronto. It was a one owner doctor's coupe. Ivan bought the car only for the nearly new set of 30 x 3 ¹/₂ tires on it he could use for his luggage trailers which he manufactured on the site.

"When I bought the car, it was sitting up on four stands made from a tree trunk. There was, of course, no tires or rims, the battery was gone and the licence expired. Still, $10.00 was a bargain. Licence plates were only two bucks at the time and ownership changed N/C with purchase of plates, a battery (used) around $5.00 for a good one, and a set of good (used) 30 x 3 ¹/₂ tires, tubes, and rims from my pal Mitch Forbes at Greenwood Auto Wreckers were about $20.00 a set, payable when you had the cash. No mechanical fitness certificate needed, no sales tax. Hardly anyone carried insurance. If you had an accident in those days, you mostly paid on the spot. The cars didn't crumble up like they do now, so $10.00 and a handshake and everything was back to normal. Gas at the Lion Station on Queen Street was generally on sale at 5 gallons for a dollar, good green bulk oil was 10 cents a quart. Also they served you gas, got down on one knee to check your oil (you had to look under the front fender to find it), filled your rad and battery if necessary and 'cleaned' your windows, all with the same rag. Free air was really free and put in by an always smiling attendant. Oh, how I wish those days were back again!

"At this time I was working for a back alley garage owned and operated by a great guy named Joe Elliot. The best all around mechanic I ever came across in my 50 years in the automotive trade. I was his one and only apprentice mechanic and he called me his man Friday, just like in Robinson Crusoe. Anyhow, I told Joe about my purchase of the '23 'T' and asked him if someday, when we weren't too busy, could he tow the car home for me. Of course the answer was yes. So, a couple of days later, we had a slack time and Joe says:

'Come on, Friday, we'll go and get your car.' I threw the tow rope in the trunk of our 'servicecar,' a 1926 Dodge coupe. This car towed cars and trucks four times her size and it never fizzed on her, so the 'T' would be a snap. Boy, was I excited. You better believe it. My First Car!

"We drove down to Ivan's, which was only a few miles from the garage, and there, in all her glory, was my car. We didn't waste time jacking it up and removing the stands. Just tied on the tow rope and one pop of the Dodge clutch, and we were on our way. Along Eastern Avenue, no problem, up Woodfield Road, no problem, then east on Queen Street, a big problem. Street car tracks. The wheels of the car got caught in the tracks and, having no horn, I had to shout to Joe to stop. We had to hang a left at Ashdale Avenue to go north to my home, but try as I may, I was caught. Period. We were discussing what to do when along came a TTC Inspector. We were holding up the east-bound Queen Street East cars and he thought there had been an accident. He produced an iron bar, such as used to manually switch the tracks, and tried to pry the 'T' wheels out of the tracks. No luck. Finally, after about six streetcars were lined up, the inspector jumped on the running board of the 'T' and hollered to Joe to tow me along to Coxwell Avenue and he would switch us north. At least we would clear the Queen Street line. I could hardly do anything for laughing at this sour-faced inspector hanging onto the 'T' with this track bar in his hand. Alas, before we got to Coxwell Avenue, I must have hit a high brick or rut and the old 'T' jumped out of the tracks and I was able to get onto Rhodes Avenue and north on a smooth paved road and home to safety.

"I drove that '23 'T' for two years and sold it to my brother Tom's friend for $11.00. In the picture of the 'T'

shown here [page 56] is Bill Reid, now a lawyer, on the deck lid, my brother Tom in the driving seat, and my late brother John on the hood. Note the licence plate number: 'PM265.' I still have it. They claimed the 'PM' stood for pull me or push me, but it really wasn't so. She ran on her own."

Gord and Lorraine Hazlett of Toronto strike a "Bonnie and Clyde" pose in front of a 1928 Nash sedan at the side of Highway 2 near Frenchman's Bay in September of 1939. The car was owned by Jim MacTavish, who frequently lent it to his friend Gord, an auto mechanic. The car needed all the help it could get, especially when going uphill. The

clutch slipped so badly, other cars frequently had to push it "over the top." But at least it ran, which is more than you could say for Jim MacTavish's previous car, a green-and-black '29 Durant roadster that Jim had bought in running condition from Greenwood Auto Wreckers for $35. A friend named Bill Tobin borrowed Jim's roadster one day to drive to a nearby fish-and-chips store. As he was going along Ashdale Avenue he revved up the engine for the benefit of two attractive young women walking along the sidewalk. A rod went right through the block, and Bill coasted to a stop around the corner. A trail of oil could be seen on the street for weeks. The old roadster went back to Greenwood Auto Wreckers and stayed there.

Optional Equipment

"Remember when drive-in shows first started? They were a boon to the family man with children. Six got in for the price of two. Dad paid for Mum and himself and four kids under 12 got in free.

"At this time, I had a '29 Buick four door sedan in lovely shape. Our family car. You who have been to these shows know the nature of problems with the kids. Well, I do too! No sooner had one relieved himself than another started bouncing on the back seat. . . . He's got to go too! Anyhow, a lot of good movies I never saw, as I was making these rush calls to the washroom. The wife says, 'I'll fix this. Next time we'll bring a jam jar.' That worked fine for a couple of times until it got kicked over by one of the kids in the excitement of Bugs Bunny, and the lid was cross-threaded. The woven rear mat had to be dried and aired. So I said, 'I'll take care of the situation myself.' I drilled a 2 inch hole in the floor and installed a 3 foot length of rad hose. I had the only '29 Buick, to my knowledge, with a built-in urinal, and not a drop was spilled from then on. As you may have already realized, my four kids were all boys."

from *The Klaxon*, the official publication of the Historical Automobile Society of Canada

WITH LOVE FROM JOE

From Joe with Love

A very dapper Joe Leonard, village jeweller from Toronto's east end, stands proudly beside a dazzling 1936 Studebaker President three-window coupe. From hubcaps to hood ornament, this car is a classic example of Art Deco styling. The company that built it was located in South Bend, Indiana, with Canadian operations in Windsor, Ontario. The Studebaker brothers got things rolling in 1852 when they went into the carriage business. The company had been in business over eighty years when the car shown here was built. Declining sales in the late 1950s put the writing on the wall; by the early sixties, the South Bend operation was at an end, and the company struggled on another four years in Hamilton, Ontario, building its final car in 1966. But when the coupe shown here was new, Studebaker gave every indication it would be around forever.

Luxury in the Depression

Few cars were farther removed from the hardships of the Great Depression than the V-16 Cadillac. Conceived in a decade that believed in endless prosperity, it was introduced at the New York Auto Show in January of 1930, just two months after the big stock market crash of '29. Riding on a 148-inch wheelbase and cooled by five vent doors on each side of its long hood, the new V-16 engine boasted 452 cubic inches cranking out a conservatively rated 165 horsepower at 3,400 rpm. Only the mighty Duesenberg was more powerful. Each bank of cylinders had its own separate carburetor and fuel supply, and the engine itself breathed through over-head valves with hydraulic tappets. The overall result was a

powerplant that was very fast, very smooth, and very quiet.

The new engine had a production run of eleven model years before declining sales brought it to an end mid-way through the 1940 model year. A total of 4,403 were sold, but nearly two-thirds of those were sold in the first year of production. It's a miracle it lasted as long as it did, especially considering that only 212 V-16s were sold between 1934 and 1938.

The 1930 Cadillac V-16 Fleetwood dual cowl phaeton seen here was photographed in a parade at the Canadian National Exhibition grounds in 1936. Toronto automotive historian Jim Brockman believes the rear seat passenger with the fancy headgear to be Herbert Alexander Bruce, who served as Lieutenant-Governor of Ontario from 1932 to 1937. What became of the car is a mystery.

Queen's Park Traffic, 1936

These cars are heading south on the west side of Queen's Park Crescent on November 21, 1936. The building in the background is Hart House on the University of Toronto campus. The late-1920s roadster in the foreground (MR602) is missing a spare tire from the left front fender, but the bracket that supported it is still sticking out of the side of the cowl. The top of the spare tire in the other front fender can be seen. Also visible is the left shoulder of someone sitting in the rumble seat, unprotected from the late November weather.

Merging Traffic

Except for the cars, the brick pavement, and the Marathon Gasoline billboard on the right, this scene has changed very little since this picture was taken on November 26, 1936. Traffic from Davenport Road enters from the right while traffic from Russell Hill Road enters from the left. The bottleneck under the CPR overpass has to work its way through the intersection at Dupont Street south of the tracks. The oval-windowed coupe in the foreground has either lost its spare tire or carries it in the trunk (not a rumble seat but a trunk, as we can tell from the placement of the handle). The car carries only one tail light, a common practice back then. Note the three cars with trunk racks, folded up and out of the way of tailgaters.

It's a Bird! It's a Plane! It's Lucky Teter!

"Lucky Teter" dazzled the crowds at the CNE grandstand with his daredevil stunts behind the wheel. He always preferred new cars, and this 1938 Plymouth sedan tells us the year this photo was taken. One of the death-defying "Hell Drivers," Teter could not get an insurance company to cover him for this kind of driving, and so he sold "Lucky Teter" souvenir coins in the grandstand to raise money for his family in case he didn't live to finish his show (these coins are highly prized collectibles today). "Lucky Teter" pulled in huge crowds in Canada and the United States, then made one jump too many. He landed short and was killed.

Sharknose at Queen and Yonge

There was no shortage of shoppers at Queen and Yonge (looking north) at 1:50 p.m. on Tuesday, April 19, 1938. Holland rose bushes sold for twenty-five cents from the store on the northwest corner, next to Eaton's, while *The Girl from the Golden West* played across the street at Loew's Theatre. An old sedan speeds through the intersection as two ladies stop in the middle of the street to let it pass. A nearly new '37 Lasalle convertible coupe eases its way around the corner. Note the step plate on the right rear fender leading to the rumble seat. Speeding into the intersection from the left is a new 1938 "Spirit of Motion" Graham with its unique "sharknose" front end. It could be purchased with an optional supercharger that boosted the horsepower of its 6-cylinder engine from 90 to 116 — enough oomph to get you through any intersection.

Richmond Street, 1939

Simpsons trucks impede the flow of traffic on Richmond
Street in 1939. The marquee for the Tivoli theatre is visible
in the background. The passenger sticking his head out of
the truck in the foreground seems eager to be included in
the photo. Judging by the sign on the windshield, the truck
is heading for the nearest race track, closely followed by a
1937 Oldsmobile sedan. A '37-'38 Chev sedan shows its hind
end to the camera while an early-1930s roadster with rumble seat, dual sidemounts, and wire wheels waits expectantly
for its owner at the side of the street. Many cars and trucks
like the ones you see here were swallowed up in the scrap
metal drive during World War Two (1939–1945).

PART THREE

From Rumble Seats to Fuel Injection, 1939-1957

When the 1930s came to an end, so did the rumble seat, with only Ford and Plymouth offering this once-popular feature, for the last time, in 1939. Running boards were on the way out too, as car bodies grew wider and turned interiors into living rooms on wheels. In February of 1942, the demands of war halted all production of civilian automobiles for over three years, and Toronto motorists faced the harsh reality of gas rationing. After the Second World War ended in 1945, the pent-up demand for new cars created a sales bonanza that kept climbing for more than a decade. Dramatic new styling, beginning in the late 1940s, combined with a tire-squealing increase in horsepower, lured a steady stream of car buyers into Toronto showrooms. By 1957, you could buy a new family-sized car with space-age tailfins or a new Corvette sports car with fuel injection. What a change from the day when Toronto's first car took to the streets nearly sixty-five years earlier!

Last Chance to Buy a New LaSalle

The LaSalle was introduced by General Motors in March 1927 to fill the price gap between Buick and Cadillac, a decision in keeping with GM President Alfred Sloan's policy of offering "a car for every price and pocketbook." It was that policy which helped General Motors become the corporate giant it is today.

During the 1930s, LaSalle sales helped Cadillac to stay afloat. In the grim Depression year of 1933, total division sales were a meagre 6,700 units, half of which were LaSalles. In 1937, combined sales were 46,000, with LaSalle accounting for 32,000 of those. But the "bean counters" at GM were sharpening the axe. The recession of 1938 cut sales figures in half, and new styling for 1939 failed to produce the anticipated results (only 23,000 LaSalles of all body styles were built that year). GM accountants kept insisting the LaSalle was pulling sales away from the more expensive and more profitable Cadillac. The LaSalle was dropped at the end of the 1940 model year, making the convertible shown here one of the last shining examples of this once-proud marque.

Dr. Wallace Lyle MacLaren was a dentist in northern Ontario who travelled over 400 miles south to Toronto to take delivery of his brand-new 1940 LaSalle Series 50 convertible coupe from Beattie Cadillac, just north of Bay and College (now Addison on Bay Ltd.). Gleaming black with red leather upholstery, it had "streamboards" instead of running boards, and it was one of only 599 built.

Dr. MacLaren's wife later took his picture with the car parked on the Ivy Lea Bridge in eastern Ontario.

On their way home to Kapuskasing, the MacLarens were driving through North Bay when another car suddenly pulled out in front of them. Dr. MacLaren slammed on the brakes so hard, he sprained his ankle. The new LaSalle hit the other car, and the MacLarens had to spend the next week in North Bay while the car was being repaired. After this accident, the car served them well until it was traded in the following year on a 1941 Cadillac.

Downtown with the Top Down

Looking west through the intersection at Bay and Adelaide in 1941, the camera from Pringle and Booth Ltd. captures a nearly new 1940 Mercury convertible coming out of a left turn to speed north on Bay Street. Note the top boot carefully snapped into place and the optional-at-extra-cost white-wall tires. Also note the sign for the Bay-Adelaide Garage in the background. Adelaide and Richmond streets carried two-way traffic until the late 1950s, when Adelaide became one-way eastbound and Richmond one-way westbound. The

18-storey Canada Permanent Trust Company Building on the southwest corner (320 Bay Street) was officially opened on April 7, 1930, and has recently undergone a complete restoration by Brookfield Developments, the new owner.

This photo is one of many taken by Pringle and Booth Ltd., professional photographers still in business in Toronto. The negatives for this picture and many others of the downtown area around 1941 were destroyed several years ago in a fire. Fortunately, prints from those negatives were stored in the Toronto Transit Commission Archives, making possible reproductions such as the one you see here.

Avenue Road Bottleneck

A great place to take pictures of cars in Toronto in 1941 was Avenue Road just south of St. Clair Avenue during the afternoon rush hour. In those days, Avenue Road shrank from four lanes to two at St. Clair, creating the bottleneck shown here (today, Avenue Road northbound shrinks from six lanes to four).

The second car in the outside lane in the foreground is a 1937 Packard 115-C 6-cylinder convertible coupe with rum-ble seat (1941 plate #465A4). A medium-green Packard identical to this one was bought new and driven for years by Ken Haggart, sportswriter with the *Toronto Telegram*. Haggart's car is now fully restored and owned by John Hillenbrand of Brossard, Quebec. It is possible that the Packard in the 1941 photo may be Ken Haggart's actual car.

Police Versus
Local Meat Market

This 1942 Dodge three-passenger business coupe was purchased new from National Motors, a Chrysler dealership on the southeast corner of Bay and Wellesley (the building was recently demolished). Mr. Morris, the new owner, chose the Dodge over a new Chevrolet because the fender design of the Chev extended into the door and created a rather large opening in the front fender whenever the door was opened (he thought snow would collect in there, making it difficult to close the door).

Mr. Morris operated Morris's Meat Market at 516 Eglinton Avenue West ("famous for tender prized meats") and painted his car in the black-and-white design shown here (he had previously owned a similarly painted '38 Chev). The Ontario Provincial Police began using this colour scheme in 1941, and a replica of cruiser number 1 (a black-and-white 1941 Chev coupe) is parked today in the OPP Lakeshore garage in Toronto. When the OPP spotted Mr. Morris's black-and-white Dodge coupe, two OPP officers entered his store in the summer of 1943 and asked him to repaint his car.

Mr. Morris refused, as was his legal right, and kept driving the car with black-and-white paint until around 1947, when he traded it in for something else.

When gas rationing was imposed during the Second World War, Mr. Morris's Dodge coupe was given an "A" sticker for its windshield, which placed it in the same category as other cars. To get more gas to make his deliveries, Mr. Morris removed the trunk lid and installed a large plywood box to convert the car into a pickup truck. He now qualified for a commercial "B" sticker, which allowed him to buy more gas. This came in especially handy when he drove out to the St.Clair-Keele area to pick up sides of beef.

Having Fun with an Old Dodge

This 1931 Dodge 6-cylinder three-window rumble-seat coupe was photographed around the summer of 1944 on the northeast side of Clarence Square, near Spadina and King, in front of a building that still stands today. The young man sitting on the fabric insert roof is Louis Harris, owner of the car. His friend in the front seat is Jack Morton, who donated the photograph. After every big rainstorm, Louis and Jack and a couple of friends usually headed down to Unwin Avenue near Cherry Beach to do some "aquaplaning" in the old Dodge. Low-lying parts of Unwin Avenue regularly became flooded to a depth of 18 inches and the Dodge would plough through at full throttle with water blowing right over the roof and onto the movers' blanket protecting the two passengers in the rumble seat who were kneeling on the seat cushion and looking back at the submerged tailpipe blowing water all over behind the car. The car usually stalled just after the floorboards began floating around inside the passenger compartment. That's when the boys climbed over the roof and onto the front fenders to open the hood and dry off the spark plug wires. Then they drove out of the water and went at it again…and again…and again….

Washing the Family Car

A father and his two sons wash the family car in the gravel driveway beside their home at 375 Glencairn Avenue in North Toronto on a sunny afternoon in the summer of 1944. The blue sticker on the windshield took the place of licence plates that year because of the shortage of metal during the Second World War. The car is a black 1940 Mercury two-door sedan purchased new for $1,200 from the Riverdale Garage, one of Toronto's largest Ford-Mercury dealers. Six years after this picture was taken, the gearshift linkage fell off in the middle of the intersection of Avenue Road and Bloor, and the car was then traded in for a new 1950 Ford.

The War Is Over!

"'We're nobody special, we're just everybody,' exclaimed the happy group on this roadster making its way down York Street this morning" (*Toronto Telegram*, Tuesday, May 8, 1945). It was V-E Day and the war in Europe was over. York Street at that time carried two-way traffic its full length from Queen Street to Lakeshore Boulevard. The use of the word "roadster" in the news item was a carryover from the days when two-door cars had side curtains (often in combi-

nation with a folding windshield). The first true American convertibles (open cars with roll-up windows) first appeared in volume in 1927. By the time this 1940 Oldsmobile was built, many convertibles came equipped with a power top.

Note the absence of a front licence plate on this car. No front licence plates were issued to Ontario motorists in 1943, 1945, 1946, or 1947 because of metal shortages caused by the war. As mentioned earlier, the 1944 "plate" was a sticker on the windshield.

Rumble-Seat Revellers

V-J Day celebrations in Toronto on August 16, 1945, included these people driving along Yonge Street at 8:30 p.m. in a 1937 Dodge convertible. This now highly collectible car is showing its age with stone chips on the front fenders, a bent front bumper guard, and rubber missing from the running board. The fender skirts would be a very hot item at flea markets today. Under the hood was a flathead 6-cylinder engine, which continued in production basically unchanged until 1960, when it was replaced by the Chrysler Corporation's new overhead-valve "Slant Six."

Saturday Afternoon Entertainment

It's the summer of 1945 at Cherry Beach, at the east end of Toronto's waterfront. Seventeen-year-old Jack Morton (now living in Willowdale) is struggling with the steering wheel of a friend's '29 DeSoto. Ken Park owned the car, but Jack did most of the driving because Ken didn't have a driver's licence. Lawrence Duncan is doing the pushing and the man with his back to the camera is Gilbert Gill ("Gilly the Ghost from coast to coast"), who collected Auburns and Cords all through the 1940s, when you could buy them off Toronto used car lots for a few hundred dollars apiece.

The DeSoto regularly ended up at the water's edge on Saturday afternoons because Jack and his friends would speed along the path through the trees to where the beach began — and then keep on going with the gas pedal to the floor. With sand flying all over, the car would travel a hundred feet or more before getting bogged down by the water's edge. It would take a good part of the afternoon to push the car back into the woods, where they would go at it all over again!

The car itself began life as a '29 DeSoto coupe, but the top was hacked off to turn it into a roadster. A bed rail had to be welded between the two windshield posts to keep the body from falling apart. The doors, not surprisingly, refused to close properly.

The vacuum tank for the DeSoto gas tank was not working, so Jack and Ken climbed over the fence of an auto wrecker at night at least a dozen times in search of a replacement tank (it didn't occur to them to fix the one they already had).

They often used a hose to siphon gas from the tank at the rear into a gallon can, the contents of which they then poured into the vacuum tank on the firewall. This supplied the carburetor with enough gas for about 5 miles — then they had to do it all over again. After emptying the can, they entertained themselves by lighting a match and igniting the fumes. POOF! In fireworks of another kind, they drove the old DeSoto through the streets of Toronto on V-J day in August 1945.

Later that summer, they brush-painted the black DeSoto a bright red, which made the car much more conspicuous to everyone, including the police, who pulled them over one night. The hydraulic brakes were defective, as were a lot of other things on the car, and the plates were removed on the spot.

Ken sold the car to Queen City Auto Wreckers on Queen Street. About six months later, Jack walked past and looked over the fence and saw the old '29 DeSoto still sitting there. The rain had washed off nearly all the red paint, making the old car the original black once more.

Ready for the
Auto Wreckers

Toronto Telegram, June 24, 1947: "Two Port Credit men narrowly escaped death or serious injury when their car plunged
40 feet into a branch of the Mimico Creek on Highway 27,
near Malton, early today.

"The men are Charles Donner, 28, of Wesley Avenue, Port
Credit, and Charles Kelley, 28, of Mississauga Road, Port
Credit.

"Provincial Constable Don Little said the two were driving south toward the Lakeshore road at 1:30 a.m. when
their car went out of control, swerved across the highway
and crashed through a guard rail, hurtling 40 feet into the
water which is about five feet deep at that point.

"The auto landed on its side. Donner was knocked unconscious by the crash. Kelley managed to grab him as the car
filled with water, pulled him out of a window and swam
with him to shore, about 15 feet away.

"Donner revived as Kelley pulled him out of the water.

"After hailing a passing motorist, who called provincial
police, the men went to the office of Dr. W. K. Fenton at
Islington. They were treated for minor injuries. 'I guess we
sure are lucky,' grinned Kelley as he ruefully felt the large
bump behind his left ear."

My Last Trip

Among the many Toronto streetcars replaced by buses over the years was car 2150, seen here in this "last-day photo" at Main and Humber streets in Weston on Monday, September 13, 1948. Someone tied the streetcar to this Model T Ford bearing the sign "To The Junkyard" – then the motorman and others posed for the camera before the car took its last run to "The Junction" and into the Roncesvalles carhouse.

The 1915 brass-rad Model T was owned by Al Laceby (seated proudly behind the wheel), who drove the car in many parades in the Weston area in the forties and fifties. Judging by the lettering on the hood – "1914–1918 C.A.F." – he may have been a veteran of the First World War. Laceby bought the car in 1927 and owned it for over forty years before selling it to area resident Cliff Love around 1970. Love sold the car a few years later, still in running condition.

Automotive historian Les Henry has estimated that two percent of all Model T Fords ever built are still around – of fifteen million, that adds up to three hundred thousand cars!

Two Old-Timers

This photo looks west from the northeast corner of Jarvis and Front streets. The old Weigh House was demolished in the 1960s, and the St. Lawrence Market building in the background was transformed into a modern structure. The still-original portion of the St. Lawrence Market on the south side of Front Street is just beyond view to the left.

The automobile you see here was featured in the *Toronto Telegram* on April 6, 1949: "In good condition and still driving around the streets is this 40-year-old auto, owned by J. W. Brock of Toronto. It is shown near another 'old timer,' the Weigh House beside St. Lawrence Market. A 1909 model Buick, the ancient car has a four-cylinder engine, and will, the owner thinks, do 50 mph — 'but I wouldn't want to try it,' he says."

By the end of the 1940s, old cars like this one were beginning to attract the attention of people who could see the financial possibilities of collecting and restoring old cars. One of these people was Ron Fawcett.

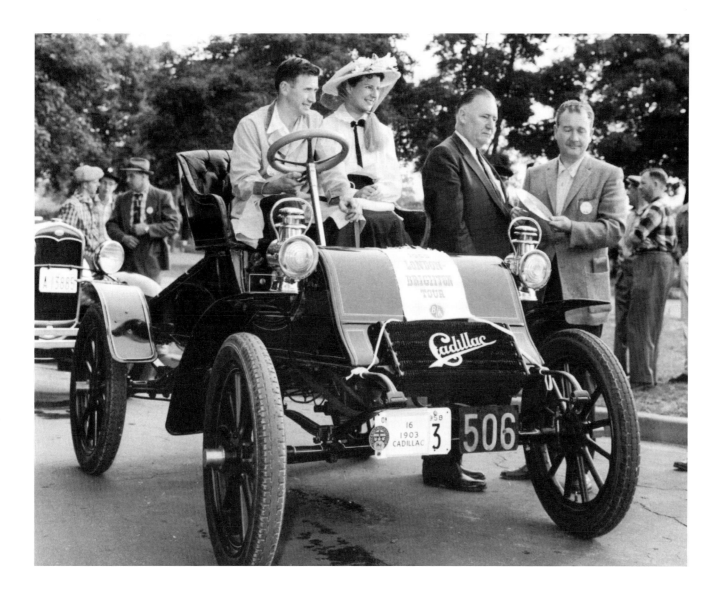

Ron Fawcett: The Man Behind a Lot of Wheels

Born in Hamilton, Ontario, in 1928, Ron Fawcett has bought, sold, repaired, and restored thousands of old cars over the past fifty years. Here he is, in 1958, behind the wheel of his 1903 Cadillac in the middle of the London-to-Brighton antique car tour across southern Ontario. This tour was first held in this province the previous year and takes its name from the London-to-Brighton Tour in England, first held in 1896 to celebrate the repeal of the "Red Flag law," which required British motorists to be preceded by a man on foot waving a red flag to warn of the car's approach.

By the early 1950s, Ron was finding hundreds of "barn-fresh" Model T Fords and other old cars in and around the Ontario countryside. Every time he brought one home, he stopped at nearly every gas station on the way to buy a gallon of gas. A crowd would gather around the old car, and somebody was sure to say they knew of another old car just like it in a barn a couple of miles away. If you have trouble finding the proverbial "old car in a barn," it's easy to understand why: Ron Fawcett got there first.

Ron won a big trophy with his '03 Cadillac at a CNE Automotive Day in the early 1950s. The car has a special place in Ron's heart: "Believe it or not, this car was the car that R. S. McLaughlin [founder of General Motors of Canada] had his first ride in — the first car that he actually had a ride in! I owned the thing, but I didn't know about this at the time. If I had known, I'd still have the car. I sold it to a man in Europe and it's gone."

Ron bought his first Model A Ford in 1942, when he was fourteen. He soon caught "Model A fever" and bought them off used car lots in and around Toronto for as little as $35 apiece, drove them home, fixed them up, and sold them for a profit. He soon became known as the "King of the Model A's."

By the mid-1950s, many of the cars Ron worked on were becoming collectors' items, and Ron became a founding member of the Antique and Classic Car Club of Canada. During these years, he searched the back roads of Ontario and found old cars in barns, swamps, and cow pastures, then trailered them home to his restoration shop in Whitby, just east of Toronto. By the mid-1960s, the work in Ron's shop was taking him all over North America in search of hard-to-find cars and parts. His son Peter and Art Carty now run the business while Ron works at home, restoring Pierce-Arrows and other vehicles, and supplying old cars for movies and television. He is now known as the "King of the Movie Cars."

And what car maker does Ron Fawcett admire the most? "Henry Ford. He's the genius who put the whole world on wheels. My only regret in life is that I never got to meet him and shake his hand."

Ron has many automotive memories:

"It was the spring of 1934 and we were living in a rented house in Hamilton in the middle of the Depression. Dad was out of work and the landlord was going to evict us on the Monday and keep our furniture for the back rent. Then, about ten o'clock on the Sunday night – I was about five years old at the time and I can remember it like yesterday – I hear CHIK, CHUK, CHIK, CHUK, and this old Model T comes into our yard, running on three cylinders.

"Then a guy rapped on the back door. Dad went to the door and the guy said: 'I understand you buy the odd old car and fix it up and sell it.'

"Dad, being an honest man, said: 'Yes, I do, but I'm financially embarrassed right now.' He sure was telling the truth. We hadn't eaten in a week!

"Then the guy with the T said: 'I don't think I've got enough gas to get my car home. That's a nice little screen door you got there. Would you be interested in trading the screen door for the car?'

"Dad never even answered him. He picked up a screwdriver, unscrewed the door, then gave him the door, the screws, *and* the screwdriver! Then the guy walked off down the street with the door under his arm.

"We weren't long scrounging some gas around the neighbourhood. Dad handed me a rubber hose and two one-gallon cans. But my Dad wasn't a nasty man. He told me if I heard a funny sucking noise at the bottom of the tank, put a little back in so the poor guy can get to work in the morning.

Ron's dad drove the "screen door" Model T for many years as a clown car in parades at country fairs and other events in and around the Whitby-Oshawa area. We see him here in the summer of 1958, exhausted and unconscious after a day of hell-raising behind the wheel of the T. When his dad passed away in 1974, Ron took the steering wheel off the T and placed it in his dad's hands so he could be buried with it. Now called "Buck 'n' Snort," that same Model T (with a new steering wheel) still entertains crowds all over southern Ontario as Ron and his wife, Huguette, in greasepaint and clown suits, drive it around with off-centre front wheels, floppy rubber running boards, barbed wire carrying juice to the spark plugs, a body that jacks itself up and down, and cleverly concealed hoses that spray water all over nearby spectators. Not bad for a car that was built over seventy years ago!

"So I got a couple of gallons and we dumped it into the tank under the front seat. By this time, my Dad had the engine running on all four cylinders. Then we packed the heavy stuff on the bottom of the back seat and piled everything else on top. It looked like a load of hay.

"Then we left as soon as we got her loaded. Headed right out of town and drove all night, just me and my Mom and Dad – and my dog.

"Dad kept the car for years, then gave it to me. I've still got it – and it still runs.

"Around 1940, I bought a second-hand bike for twelve dollars and wore out ten sets of tires delivering papers and groceries. Then I fixed it up with chrome accessories and sold it for fifty bucks. I rebuilt lots of bikes and made money on every one.

"Then I bought my first car. It was a '28 Model A soft-top sport coupe. That was in 1942 and I was going on fourteen. The farmer wanted fifty bucks for it and I got it for thirty-five. I ran out of gas at the end of his driveway, so I waited till he went down to feed the pigs, then I helped myself to some of his tractor gas. I drove five miles home along the roadbed of Highway 401 – it was under construction at the time.

"I had no driver's licence, no licence plates, and no insurance, but I did have a broken piston. The rear end locked up on me on the way home and I had to rock the car back and forth to get it going again.

"Dad ordered me off the property as soon as I got it home. Said I was too young to have a car. I took it over to Howard Sleep's place – he was ten years older and he was an auto mechanic. That's where I worked on it all that summer. I replaced the broken piston, then put in all new rings and ground the valves. I hung a chain from a tree to raise the back end so I could replace the crown and pinion.

"Then I replaced all the rods operating the four wheel brakes. The transmission was fine and all the lights worked. I sanded the whole body and painted it carefully with a brush. Howard helped me with all this.

"The car had a trunk and I needed a rumble seat for double dates. So I found an abandoned Model A coupe with a rumble seat in a nearby swamp, and I had to lay down a bunch of planks and logs so I could crawl out to it. I took the rumble seat, the hinges, the hand rails, the step plates, the bumpers, and everything else I could strip off it.

"George Morrison was a couple of years older than me and had his driver's licence. We drove all over in that Model A of mine with George behind the wheel in the daytime and me behind the wheel at night, when the police would have trouble seeing how young I was. We dated two sisters and I sat in the rumble seat with the younger one at the drive-in. The older one kept looking back at us, so I finally closed the lid for some privacy. There was no chance of smothering because the body was full of rust holes."

Ron bought his first Model A roadster off a used car lot near St. Clair and Dufferin in 1944, but that's another story.

■ ───────────────────────────

One of Ron's favourite personal cars from the early days was this yellow 1950 Monarch convertible with wide whitewalls and fender skirts. Ron worked as a mechanic at Seaway Motors in Oshawa when he owned this car, and one night in 1956, while he was working late, another fellow in the shop offered to wash the Monarch for him. To clean the rear whitewalls, Ron's co-worker removed the fender skirts, jacked up the rear end, started the engine, put it in low gear, and began soaping the rear tires while they were turning.

Meanwhile, Ron was working on something else by the wall in front of his car. Suddenly, the jack slipped and Ron's car began speeding across the floor with no one in it. Ron jumped out of the way, but his arm got caught between the wall and the left front fender, nearly slicing his hand off. A hair-raising 100-mile-an-hour drive to the Oshawa hospital saved Ron's hand in the nick of time.

The Featherstone-Brady Mercurys

Because of the shortage of new cars after the Second World War, the demand for good used cars remained very strong through the late 1940s. Two Toronto high-school students decided to make some extra money buying and selling used cars.

Jim Featherstone was born in Toronto on January 8, 1927, and grew up on Charles Street near Church and Bloor. He attended Northern Vocational School at 851 Mount Pleasant Road (now Northern Secondary School), where he met Brian Brady in his architectural drafting class. The two boys became best friends. Brian, seen here behind the wheel, had a passion for old cars and had already bought and sold sever-

al immaculate open-bodied 1936 Fords, including a roadster, phaeton, and convertible sedan. He was now ready to turn his attention to another very popular used car in Toronto in the late 1940s: the '40 Mercury convertible. There were lots of them around, many of them still in excellent condition and still being driven by their original owners. Brian and Jim decided to team up for fun and profit, and the routine went something like this: they would see a '40 Merc convertible rolling by on the street, write down the licence number, get the name and address of the owner from the Motor Vehicles Department at Queen's Park, then phone the owner and offer to buy the car. Sometimes a deal was struck right away, and sometimes the owner would phone back in a few days or a few weeks, ready to sell. Jim and Brian usually paid about $850 for each car, then spent about $50 cleaning it up for resale.

They had an arrangement with Tony and Vince Barracco, who ran a used car lot on Bloor Street West near Shaw Street. Each '40 Merc convertible that Jim and Brian picked up was put on the lot and sold on consignment, usually for about $1,200. The $300 profit was split three ways: $100 each to Jim and Brian and $100 for Barracco Motors. Tony and Vince liked the arrangement very much and asked Jim and Brian to bring in more cars.

And bring in more cars they did. A total of fifteen '40 Mercury convertibles passed through their hands in a couple of years. They owned as many as three of them at once, and where to keep them sometimes posed a problem. Jim's parents' house had no driveway or garage, and he often had to rent garages around the neighbourhood or park the cars on the street. Some of the cars needed new clutches, and that was just about the only mechanical repair that Jim and

Brian had to make. They never had any trouble with the vacuum-operated power tops, even though these cars were nearly ten years old. However, occasionally they had to replace the tops, and a fellow who worked at Canadian Tire installed them at home for $100.

Brian and Jim worked through a finance company to purchase their '40 Mercs until they had accumulated enough profit to buy the cars outright. Two of the '40 Mercs became "keepers," which they drove as their personal transportation. Brian had a black ragtop, and Jim's was navy blue. As other '40 Mercs passed through their hands, they took the best parts off each car and put them on their own. That way, they each ended up with a pair of super-mint '40 Mercury convertibles – restored on the instalment plan.

As the forties turned into the fifties, Brian and Jim shifted their attention to the new "shoebox" Ford convertibles and later to the early Corvettes and two-seater Thunderbirds. The '40 Mercs were all sold off, but still live on in memories and photographs.

It's a Honey!

This new Mercury convertible appeared in an ad placed by Yonge-Eglinton Motors in the 1951 yearbook of North Toronto Collegiate Institute, located just north of Yonge and Eglinton at 70 Roehampton Avenue. The school celebrated its seventy-fifth anniversary in 1987. Yonge-Eglinton Motors served the North Toronto area for many years as a Mercury-Lincoln-Meteor dealer from its garage and showroom at 2340 Yonge Street. The property today forms part of the Yonge-Eglinton Centre, a shopping mall with eighty-five stores.

According to *The Ford V-8 Album,* the Ford Motor Company built 6,759 Mercury convertibles for 1951 – and they were available in a dazzling array of colours: Black, Banning Blue Metallic, Everglade Green, Mission Gray, Coventry Green Gray, Sheffield Green, Tomah Ivory, and (exclusive to the convertible) Vassar Yellow.

The one pictured here has a radio, a spotlight, and a fancy hood ornament. The spotlight is described in 1951 Ford and Mercury sales literature as an accessory that "is not only a beauty but a real friend-in-need when you're trying to pick out a road sign at night, find a house number, or watch the edge of winding and hilly roads. A turn of its handsome plastic pistol-grip handle shoots the beam wherever you want it, and lights up objects hundreds of feet away."

The Mercury was the brainchild of Henry Ford's son, Edsel, who wanted a medium-priced car to fill the gap between the Ford Deluxe and the Lincoln-Zephyr. It was introduced in the fall of 1938 as a '39 model and was available in four body styles: two-door sedan, four-door sedan, coupe, and convertible coupe (a very rare convertible sedan was added to the Mercury line for 1940). It was Edsel Ford who selected the name of the new car (named after the Roman god of swiftness) from a list of at least one hundred suggestions, including Comet, Consul, Corsair, Falcon, Ford XL, and Ranger, all of which later appeared on other Ford products.

The freshly scrubbed and squeaky-clean teenagers sitting in the new '51 Mercury convertible shown here could not afford to buy such a car – but their parents could, and they were the ones this ad was aimed at.

Eight years later, a different breed of teenager swarmed around this car (or ones just like it) in summertime hangouts like Wasaga Beach or Grand Bend. No more need to ask Mom or Dad for the car when you could buy one for yourself for just a few hundred bills. The one seen here has all the obligatory embellishments of a '51 Merc ragtop in the late fifties: fender skirts, twin deck aerials, danglements hanging from the rear-view mirror, a guitar strummer sitting on the folded top, and "RUTH" and "KURT" lovingly taped to the rear bumper.

Five Cars Into One

In 1953, Jack Morton of Willowdale bought a 1934 Ford cabriolet (two-door with folding top and roll-up windows) from a used car lot on the south side of Queen Street just east of Sherbourne for $90 (licence number 5A675). It was nice and clean on the inside, with original red leatherette and the original "mail slot" glass rear window. The motor wasn't running, so Jack bought another '34 Ford cabriolet in Uxbridge from the owner of the local movie theatre (1951 plate 9Z957). It had been off the road for two years, had no top, and was missing one rear fender — but the motor was good. Jack yanked it out and dropped it into cabriolet No. 1, then traded that car for one of the first Munroe fibreglass motorboats from London, Ontario, with a 12-horsepower Elto motor.

The parts left over from cabriolet No. 2 came in handy when Jack bought No. 3 soon after from someone in Leaside for $25. It had no front fenders, but Jack began joining Nos. 2 and 3 together to make one good car. Then he found cabriolet No. 4 (plate number 600K4), also from Leaside and also for $25. It had a plastic rear window and no motor (it had had a Caproff racing motor from Caproff Garage on Brunswick Avenue but that had been taken out and put into something else).

Car No. 4 was actually a better car than Nos. 2 or 3, so

Jack parked 2 and 3 in his back yard and cannibalized them for parts for 4. He was busy putting a '49 Mercury engine into 4 when he found No. 5. It was a better car than all the other four put together (and Jack was trying to put them all together), but it had been taken apart by Ross Cromb, brother of the stock car driver, so Jack had to bring it home in pieces. Cabriolet No. 5 really did turn out to be the best of the lot. Jack finished it off, put whitewalls on it, and proudly drove it in the Elks Motorcade at the CNE in 1955.

And what happened to it after that? Well, Jack later traded it, minus engine, to Cliff Love for a '34 Ford three-window coupe, also minus engine. Cliff ran the cabriolet with a Chrysler engine, then sold the car to a fellow in Malton around 1957. And that's when Jack and Cliff lost track of it.

Only in Canada

Highlighting the display of the 1953 cars from Ford of Canada at the CNE Automotive Building was this dazzling Monarch convertible, dressed up and ready to go in whitewalls, fender skirts, and rocker panel mouldings. The Monarch was first introduced with the 1946 models as a Canadian version of the Mercury, which was also built and sold in Canada. The Monarch name reflected Canada's close ties with Britain, as did the crown-shaped keyhole cover just below the door handle. The giant V-8 insignia above the car had been a Ford trademark since 1932, when Henry Ford had introduced the first V-8 engine in the low-priced field. It proved to be a huge commercial success, but its days were numbered when this photo was taken. The horsepower race of the 1950s forced a change in the design of the combustion chamber, and in 1954, in the United States, both Ford and Mercury were powered by a new overhead-valve V-8. Canadian Mercurys and Monarchs were also powered by the new engine, but Canadian-built Fords in 1954 (and their Canada-only companion car, the Meteor) had to settle for the now out-dated flathead engines in order to use up the leftovers. These cars had to wait until 1955 before getting the new state-of-the-art power plant.

Lakeshore Bottleneck

Before the opening of the Gardiner Expressway in the late 1950s, eastbound traffic on the Queen Elizabeth Way had to merge with Lakeshore Boulevard traffic just west of the Humber River Bridge, creating the rush-hour bottleneck shown here on the morning of Thursday, September 30,

1954. (An artist at the time added the six bottlenecks above the traffic to the left.) The letters "ER" near the top of the lampposts stand for "Elizabeth Regina," wife of King George VI, who gave her name to the new highway when the royal couple visited Canada in the spring of 1939. Some American tourists at that time thought the letters were erected in honour of Eleanor Roosevelt.

The car at the lower left (licence number 79C99) is a Raymond Loewy-designed Studebaker Starlight coupe, first introduced in the 1953 model year and hailed then, as now, as one of the finest automotive designs of that decade. The driver was probably a man in a business suit, judging by the hand and shirt cuff resting on the back of the front seat.

Other cars creeping along nearby include, from left to right, a Studebaker sedan, an Austin A40, a '54 Meteor sedan, a '53 Pontiac sedan, a '54 Chev sedan, a '49-'52 Chev two-door with spotlight, fender skirts, and chrome gas lid trim, a '54 Buick Special, and a two-tone 1940 Chev coach. The Regent gas station in the background is trying to lure customers in with its exotic tile roof and little flags flapping in the breeze.

How many readers recognize the ghostly outline of the building faintly visible in the background? You're looking at the now-demolished Palace Pier, a popular big-band-era dance hall that sparked many Hogtown romances.

Hazel Hits Toronto

On a rainy night in October 1954, Hurricane Hazel roared through Toronto and left a trail of death and destruction behind it. Rivers, streams, and creeks burst their banks as more than one billion litres of water fell on Greater Toronto.

Among the cars that felt Hazel's wrath was the 1946–48 Mercury "114" four-door sedan seen here beside the Humber River, looking west from south of the Scarlett Road Bridge on October 17, 1954. It's a Canadian Mercury on the 114-inch Ford wheelbase (all U.S. Mercurys had a 118-inch wheelbase and slightly different front end styling). This Mercury carries several accessories popular at that time: an outside sun visor, fender skirts, a fancy after-market hood ornament, and a curb guide sticking up from each front fender.

Bloor Viaduct, 1956

Taken thirty-eight years after the Prince Edward Viaduct was completed, this 1956 photo was used by the TTC to demonstrate the need for an east-west Bloor-Danforth subway line. Fortunately, the viaduct had been built with a lower level for this very purpose, and that foresight saved taxpayers millions of dollars by the time the subway opened in 1966. The vehicles stuck here in bumper-to-bumper traffic represent a typical cross-section of what you would see on Toronto streets in the mid-1950s: a Volkswagen van, a '55 Chevrolet 6-cylinder (no V-8 insignia on the hood), a '56 Chrysler sedan with the "Forward Look" tailfins, a GMC pickup truck, a pair of "shark-tooth" Buick grilles, and a '40 Ford coupe.

At the End of Her Nozzle

Long before self-serve gas stations became popular, Barb Pickard of the *Toronto Telegram* decided to learn how to pump gas, and "the whole lesson took only 15 minutes." The customer's car at the end of her nozzle is a '57 Chev station-wagon sold by Ken-Clair Motors of Toronto. All Chevrolets that year had the gas filler cap cleverly concealed inside the tailfin on the driver's side. The year before, it was inside the left rear tail-light housing. For 1958, it was camouflaged inside a body panel between the trunk lid and the rear bumper. On the '59 and '60 Chev, it was hidden behind the rear licence plate. Working at a gas station back then was a real challenge, especially if you were new on the job. Some pump attendants, not wishing to reveal their ignorance, ran their hands all over the car's rear end till something popped open.

Nearly 300 Horses Under the Hood

Toronto Telegram, Sept. 12, 1957: "These six sleek-looking models took part in the fashion show of sports clothes and sports cars sponsored by the merchants of the Don Mills shopping centre. From the left are Jackie Chapman, Linda Shreve, Marg Jewitt, Leslie Sniderman, and Dorothy Atkinson, all residents of the area. The sixth model is the classy Chevrolet Corvette sports car."

Fuel injection was new for 1957 (see insignia on fender cove) and boosted this Corvette's horsepower to a tire-squealing 283 – one horsepower per cubic inch.

Special Thanks

Many people have helped to make this book possible. I wish to thank Jack Philips, Doug Mills, and the staff at Mills and Hadwin ("Selling Cars Since 1922") for providing the photographs and stories that started the research on this nearly three years ago. I also wish to thank the many people on staff at archives in and around Toronto for their guidance and encouragement: Ted Wickson at the Toronto Transit Commission Archives; Nancy Hurn at the Metro Toronto Archives; Vic Russell and Steve MacKinnon at the City of Toronto Archives; Linda Cobban and Karen McGoogan at the CNE Archives; Pat Stephenson at the Canadian Tire Archives; Ron Grantz at the Detroit Public Library; Sandy Notarianni at the Ford Motor Company of Canada Archives; Sonja Lindegger at the *Globe and Mail* Archives; Alan Walker at the Metropolitan Toronto Reference Library; Linda Moon at Northern District Library; Christine Niarchos-Bourolias at the Ontario Archives; Pat Curran at the Ontario Motor League Archives; Barbara Craig and Dennis Skinner at the York University Archives; the staff at the National Archives in Ottawa; and David Monaghan, curator of Land Transportation at the National Museum of Science and Technology, also in Ottawa.

Many individuals assisted with rare photographs and information, both technical and historical: John Anderson, Glenn Baechler, Julian Bernard, Jim Brockman, Lloyd Brown, Bob Burton, Grant Cairns, Paul Calderone, Don Cockburn, Bruce Cole, John Robert Colombo, Derek Coomber, Paul Denter, Earl Domm, Eddy Edwards, Eric Edwards, Ron and Huguette Fawcett (and all the gang at Fawcett Motors in Whitby, especially Peter Fawcett and Art Carty), Jim Featherstone, Paul Fernley, Mike Filey, Bill Forsythe, Larry Gooch, Gord Hazlett, Jack Heib, Ron Hill, John Hillenbrand, Art James, Vern Kipp, Stuart Lazier and Dale Churley of the Enterprise Property Group, Cliff Love, Ron Miller, Jack Morton, Charles Neville, Wayne Plunkett, Steve Premock Jr., Steve Premock Sr., Don Ritchie, Ted Samis, John Sebert, Roderick Sergiades, George Skinner, Jeff Smith, Robert M. Stamp, George Stevens, Fred Sweet, Keith Toppin, Peter Van Dyk, Bill Vance of the *Toronto Star*; Doug Wardle, Chris Whillans, Bill Wozney, Tom Zaruk, and R. Perry Zavitz.

A special vote of thanks goes to Bill Frankling, Susan Hughes, John Thompson, and Doris Tucker of the East York Historical Society; Erin Leckie of the *East York Observer*; Scott James, managing director of the Toronto Historical Board; Howard Hutt of the Electric Vehicle Association of Canada (EVAC); Mike Foley and Ken Morrell of the Canadian Automotive Museum in Oshawa; the staff at Toronto Black & White Photo Lab Inc.; and editorial staff of *The Klaxon* (published by the Historical Automobile Society of Canada) and *The Reflector* (published by the Antique and Classic Car Club of Canada).

An extra special "thank you" goes to Murray McEwan and Murray Cutler, who publish the twice-monthly *Old Autos,* a newspaper that many of its readers have described as "the best thing that's ever happened to the old car hobby in Canada" (1-800-461-3457).

My brother, John (who publishes bicycle maps), played a very special role in pulling everything together. He introduced me to John Denison of the Boston Mills Press, and the result of that meeting is the book you are now reading. To my wonderfully patient wife, Brenda, to my brother, John, and to John Denison, Noel Hudson, Linda Gustafson, and all the staff at the Boston Mills Press/Stoddart, my sincere and heartfelt thanks for making a dream come true.

Calling All Cars!

If you have any old photos of cars in your family album, and would like to see them published in a future volume, please send photocopies, along with any interesting stories, to:

> Bill Sherk
> c/o The Boston Mills Press
> 132 Main Street
> Erin, Ontario
> N0B 1T0

Bibliography

Abbott, Elizabeth. editor-in-chief. *Chronicle of Canada*. Montreal: Chronicle Publications, 1990.

Auto Editors of Consumer Guide. *50 Years of American Automobiles, 1939-1989*. New York: Beekman House, 1989.

Auto Editors of Consumer Guide. *Ford: The Complete History*. Lincolnwood, Illinois: Publications International Ltd., 1990.

Automobile Quarterly, ed. *General Motors: The First 75 Years*. New York: Crown Publishers, Inc., 1983.

Bagnato, Sharon, and Shragge, John, ed. *Footpaths to Freeways: The Story of Ontario's Roads*. Ministry of Transportation and Communications, 1984.

Brown, Ian. *Free-wheeling*. Toronto: Harper & Collins, 1989.

Butler, Don. *The History of Hudson*. Sarasota, Florida: Crestline Publishing, Co., 1982.

Casteele, Dennis. *The Cars of Oldsmobile*. Sarasota, Florida: Crestline Publishing Co., 1981

Centennial College Press, ed. *The Golden Years of East York*. The Borough of East York, 1976.

Collins, Robert. *A Great Way To Go*. Toronto: Ryerson Press, 1969.

Colombo, John Robert. *Colombo's Canadian References*. Toronto: Oxford University Press, 1976.

Dammann, George H. *Seventy Years of Buick*. Sarasota, Florida: Crestline Publishing Co., 1973.

Dammann, George H. *75 Years of Chevrolet.* Sarasota, Florida: Crestline Publishing Co., 1986.

Dammann, George H. *The Cars of Lincoln-Mercury.* Sarasota, Florida: Crestline Publishing Co., 1987.

Durnford, Hugh, and Baechler, Glenn. *Cars of Canada.* Toronto: McClelland & Stewart Limited, 1973.

Eaves, Edward and Burger, Dan. *Great Car Collections of the World.* New York: Gallery Books, 1986.

Fenster, J. M. *Packard: The Pride.* Kutztown, Pennsylvania: Automobile Quarterly Publication, 1989.

Filey, Mike. *Mount Pleasant Cemetery: An Illustrated Guide.* Toronto: Firefly Books Ltd., 1990.

Filey, Mike. *Not a One-Horse Town.* Toronto: Firefly Books Ltd., 1990.

Filey, Mike. *Passengers Must Not Ride on the Fenders.* Toronto: Green Tree Publishing Company Ltd., 1974.

Filey, Mike. *Toronto Sketches,* "The Way We Were." Toronto: Dundurn Press, 1992.

Flink, James J. *America Adopts the Automobile, 1895-1910.* Cambridge, Massachusetts: The MIT Press, 1970.

Fryer, Mary Beacock, and Humber, Charles J., co-editors. *Loyal She Remains: A Pictorial History of Ontario.* Toronto: United Empire Loyalists' Association of Canada, 1984.

Guillet, Edwin C. *The Story of Canadian Roads.* Toronto: University of Toronto Press, 1966.

Hall, Asa E., and Langworth, Richard M. *The Studebaker Century.* Contoocook, New Hampshire: Dragonwyck Publishing Inc., 1983.

Jacobs, Timothy, and Debolski, Tom. *The Pictorial Treasury of Classic American Automobiles.* London: Bison Books Ltd., 1989.

Jones, Donald. *Fifty Tales of Toronto.* Toronto: University of Toronto Press, 1992.

Kluckner, Michael. *Toronto: The Way It Was.* Toronto: Whitecap Books Ltd., 1988.

Langworth, Richard M. *World of Cars.* New York: Automobile Quarterly, 1971.

Langworth, Richard, and Norbye, Jan. *The Complete History of Chrysler Corporation, 1924-1985.* New York: Beekman House, 1985.

Langworth, Richard. *The Great American Convertible.* New York: Beekman House, 1988.

Mackay, Claire. *The Toronto Story.* Toronto: Annick Press Ltd., 1990.

McCall, Walter M. P. *80 Years of Cadillac-LaSalle.* Sarasota, Florida: Crestline Publishing Co., 1988.

McCoppin, Bob, ed. *The V-8 Album.* San Leandro, California: The Early Ford V-8 Club of America, 1985

McPherson, Thomas A. *The Dodge Story.* Osceola, Wisconsin: Motorbooks International, 1992.

Ritchie, Don. *North Toronto.* Erin, Ontario: The Boston Mills Press, 1992.

Russell, Vic. *Toronto Flashbacks, Volume 1.* Toronto: Firefly Books Ltd., 1989.

Saturday Evening Post. *The Automobile Book.* Indianapolis: The Curtis Publishing Co., 1985.

Sherk, William. *500 Years of New Words.* Toronto: Doubleday Canada Ltd., 1983.

Stamp, Robert M. *QEW: Canada's First Superhighway.* Erin, Ontario: The Boston Mills Press, 1987.

Stevens, Robert Jay, ed. *Cars and Parts.* Published monthly. Sidney, Ohio: Amos Press Inc.

Wise, David Burgess, ed. *The Illustrated Encyclopedia of Automobiles.* Secaucus, New Jersey: Chartwell Books Inc., 1979.

Withrow, John, ed. *Once Upon a Century: 100 Year History of the 'Ex'.* Toronto: J. H. Robinson Publishing Ltd., 1978.

Wood, Jonathan. *Great Marques of America.* London: Octopus Books, 1986.

Woudenberg, Paul R. *Ford in the Thirties.* Los Angeles: Peterson Publishing Co., 1976.

Credits

For additional information on photo sources, please contact the author care of the publisher.

About the Author

BILL SHERK was born in Toronto in 1942 and has been crazy about old cars for as long as he can remember. While growing up in southern Ontario, Bill worked at a gas station, a used car lot, a chrome-plating company, and a Buick-Pontiac dealership – and he and his brother operated a very successful car-polishing business in the days of the big tailfins.

Bill majored in history at the University of Toronto and has taught that subject to high school students for over twenty-five years. The author of three books on the origin of words, Bill is a popular keynote speaker and has been interviewed more than three hundred times on radio and television in Canada and the United States. A former activities director of the Antique and Classic Car Club of Canada, a current member of the Historical Automobile Society of Canada, and a regular columnist for *Old Autos* newspaper, Bill has owned and driven old cars for thirty years.

The car he wishes he had never sold ("I still dream about it") was a customized 1940 Mercury convertible with a triple-carb '57 Chev V-8 under the hood. Bill is currently searching for that very same car he sold three decades ago, with phone calls to locations as far away as Florida, California, and Argentina.

His philosophy of life: "Keep your top down, your engine running, your foot on the gas, and your hand on the wheel."

He currently lives in Toronto with his wife, Brenda.